THE POCKET IDIOT'S GUIDE TO

Dog Tricks

by Sarah Hodgson

alpha books

A Division of Macmillan General Reference USA
A Pearson Education Macmillan Company
1633 Broadway, New York, NY 10019

To Aunt Carolyn and Uncle John, for all the pats on the head.

©1999 by Sarah Hodgson

THE POCKET IDIOT'S GUIDE TO & Design are registered trademarks of Macmillan USA.

Macmillan General Reference books may be purchased for business or sales promotional use. For information please write: Special Markets Department, Macmillan Publishing USA, 1633 Broadway, New York, NY 10019-6785.

International Standard Book Number: 1-58245105-2

01   00   99   4   3   2   1

Interpretation of the printing code: the rightmost number of the first series of numbers is the year of the book's printing; the rightmost number of the second series of numbers is the number of the book's printing. For example, a printing code of 99-1 shows that the first printing occurred in 1999.

Printed in the United States of America

Alpha Development Team

Publisher
Kathy Nebenhaus

Editorial Director
Gary M. Krebs

Managing Editor
Bob Shuman

Marketing Brand Manager
Felice Primeau

Acquisitions Editor
Jessica Faust

Development Editors
Phil Kitchel, Amy Zavatto

Assistant Editor
Georgette Blau

Production Team

Editors
Dominique De Vito, Beth Adelman

Production Editor
Faunette Johnston

Copy Editor
Diana Francoeur

Cover Designer
Mike Freeland

Cartoons
Judd Winick

Designer
Scott Cook and Amy Adams of DesignLab

Indexer
Nadia Ibrahim

Production Team
Melissa Auciello-Brogan, Laura Goetz, Sean Monkhouse

Contents

Introduction

Why a tricks book dedicated to idiots? Well, don't take the idiot part personally—I didn't pick the title. But there's been such hoopla over the original *The Complete Idiot's Guide to Choosing, Raising, and Training a Dog* (I wrote that one, too!) that the publishers thought it natural that I should follow up with a more lighthearted, fun-loving version.

Aside from writing the first *Idiot's Guide* for dogs, I'm a dog maniac who for years has been trying to take the edge off of serious training and inject the whole process with a little fun. After all, isn't one of the primary reasons we share our lives with dogs to enjoy their company while they help us loosen our grip on this no-nonsense, career-driven world? Don't get me wrong! I'm not negating the whole training process. After all, I am a dog trainer, and basic lessons are essential to let your dog know who's in charge. But once you've made that point, you can lighten up.

Though I'm something of a stickler in my obedience techniques, games and tricks have few rules. Lessons should be short, quick, and fun. And, unlike formal training where I limit the treats and toy rewards to keep your dog's focus on you, I encourage food lures, rewards, and praise when teaching tricks and fun.

Are there any limitations to joining in the fun described herein? No! Of course, there are nearly two-hundred-some-odd pages here dedicated to games and tricks, and it's likely not every page will be for you and your dog. But that many pages leaves plenty of room for a whole array of games and tricks for the everyday dog and owner. Every dog can learn to do something.

So let the fun begin! Like my other *Idiot's Guide,* you can read this book cover to cover, or surf the table of contents and create your own starting point. I've arranged the chapters in order of complexity: simple stuff first, then fancy.

What I Do All Day

Writing is not my day job. In real life I'm a dog trainer. I've been in the business of helping dogs and people for nearly twelve years, and I've often said that no one has it better; I'm earning a living at what I love to do. I feel pretty blessed!

Activities in my day vary between writing, private classes, group lessons, puppy classes, and aggression rehab—no two days are ever quite the same. There is a common theme, however, that runs through everything I do. I insist that my clients lighten up and teach their dogs something they'll enjoy. A Poodle, for example, must learn to dance. A retriever needs to fetch. Bichon Frises love their parlor tricks. Huskies want to pull a sled, herders love to herd, and so on.

Though I don't have a résumé with names like Lassie, Benji, and more modern television stars like Eddie from *Frasier* and Murray from *Mad About You,* I do have a history of igniting the imagination and motivation of dog owners to discover the magic and fun that twinkles in their dog's eyes, and to make the most of it.

Sharing your life with a dog shouldn't be a militaristic venture, selfishly designed around what you want your dog to do. Owning a dog is about joining two different species, two different spirits, in a way that will make the world better for both.

Decoding the Text

Since this is an *Idiot's Guide,* I will assume you know nothing. Please don't think I'm patronizing you if I explain a term you've known for years, but I don't want to leave anyone out in the cold. Teaching dogs brings us together as a family, so be supportive.

Some of the cool extras in reading (and writing) this book are the sidebar boxes that are sprinkled throughout the text. They're added to draw your attention to important information, or just facts that are fun to know.

Sarah Says

These *Sarah Says* tips simplify each process and clue you in to shortcuts or points you really must remember. They may also highlight how to handle dogs with special characteristics.

Hand Signals

These boxes explain the silent signals you can teach your dog, so you can put him through his paces without saying a word.

Grrr

Don't forget to read the *Grrr* warning boxes! These will caution you about common errors, dangerous habits, and things you should avoid.

Trademarks

All terms mentioned in this book that are known to be or are suspected of being trademarks or service marks have been appropriately capitalized. Alpha Books and Macmillan General Reference cannot attest to the accuracy of this information. Use of a term in this book should not be regarded as affecting the validity of any trademark or service mark.

Chapter 1

Performance Prerequisites

In This Chapter

➤ Learning to speak Doglish

➤ Outfitting the well-dressed dog

➤ The Magic Seven commands

Before you teach that dog of yours how to serve you breakfast in bed, you must make sure you can get his attention. Otherwise, he'll be the one teaching you tricks—ever see the owner-chasing-the-dog routine? It's hysterical, but very unsafe. Don't be scared; we're not going for show ring Obedience. Just the basics, boiled down to seven foundation commands I call the *Magic Seven*.

To be a fair and fun teacher you'll also need to master Doglish, your dog's native language. Until you learn to think *with* and not *against* your dog, you can't teach him properly. It's impossible for your dog to be human, no matter how much you work together. So how do you talk doglish? It's quite an adventure.

Doglish

We speak English. Our dogs speak Doglish. To be a good teacher, you must put yourself in their paws. Words don't carry the same weight; lengthy explanations leave them puzzled. Doglish consists of three simple elements: eye contact, body language, and tone.

Eye Contact

My Aunt Polly always says you can read the attraction two people have for one another by watching their eyes. Dogs aren't much different. If yours looks to you with eyes that are trusting and eager, you'll have no trouble teaching your dog anything. If you can't get a blink, you'll have to do some preliminary "respect" work, as outlined later in this chapter in the section called "The Magic Seven."

Body Language

Body language is a funny thing. As a species, we humans often overlook its power to communicate. Picture this: You're trying to teach your dog to jump through a hoop. Every time he gets to the hoop, however, he runs around it. Poor thing—he's a little nervous. You try again, but he dodges. You squeeze through yourself several times, saying, "See? Like this." Now he thinks you've lost your mind. You get frustrated. Your body tenses, eyes bulge, hands clench. Now he has a reason to avoid the hoop.

Sarah Says

Imagine a peacock, beautiful and proud, chest out, confident and in control. When giving your dog a direction or command, throw your shoulders back and stand tall like a peacock. Tell your friends and family about this peacock position and start strutting your stuff!

Stand up straight and make eye contact with your dog. It's about respect.

Training calls for a relaxed and patient body posture. I call it the *peacock position:* Stand upright and proud.

Tone

Tone is a huge part of the training process. If you yell at your dog, you'll either freak him out or look like a fool, depending on his personality profile. If you speak sweetly, you'll encourage playfulness.

To encourage your dog's attention, there is only one tone to use: the directive tone. It's clear, direct, and nonthreatening. Don't worry though, it's easy to master. Just use your regular voice with an ounce of over-enunciation. Think of your dog as a two-year-old learning his first two-syllable word. After your dog learns a particular behavior, you'll be able to whisper commands. But in the beginning, speak clearly.

Attitude

Attitude is everything. If your dog thinks you're cool, you can teach him anything he's physically capable of learning. By nature, dogs relate to a hierarchical system where one leader rules over all.

What determines who's boss? Not Rambo-like fighting power, but mental stamina. Leaders keep their heads while others all about them are unnerved. When there is confusion, all look to the head honcho for stability. The leader directs, structures, and reassures. For any type of training to be effective, you need to assume the roll of leader. Let's start.

Sarah Says

Got a multiperson household? A whole brood perhaps? You'll need to help everyone establish a hierarchy that starts with two-legged critters and ends with four-legged ones.

Outfitting Your Dog

If your dog hasn't had any training, or if he needs some brushing up, you'll need a quick refresher course before you move on. For one thing, your dog will need to be well-mannered on a leash and responsive to basic commands. Fortunately, you don't need to be a brain surgeon to master this stuff. Before we start, though, you need to outfit your dog with the right collar and leash.

Sarah Says

Every dog must wear a buckle collar with identification tags at all times. Whether your dog is two months old or two years, two pounds or two hundred, find her a nice collar and attach those tags.

Training Collars

The buckle collar is not to be confused with a training collar. The training collar is used exclusively when your dog is on a leash. The only dogs exempt are toy breeds and puppies under sixteen weeks of age, because their neck muscles are too weak for a training collar.

The Original Training Collar

I call this the original because it has been around the longest. It has some other names too, like a chain or choke collar, though if used properly it should never choke your dog. Choking and restraint only aggravate problems. Most people don't know that it is the sound of the collar, *not* the restraint, that teaches. A jingle of the chain is all it takes. I know everyone would rather use this collar properly than hear their dog hacking during walks, but most people don't know how to make the darn thing work.

Original training collar

To start with, make sure you put on the collar properly. If put on backward, this collar will cause your dear doggy lots of discomfort. Fitted improperly, the links will catch in a viselike hold around your dog's neck and do what the collar is not suppose to do—choke.

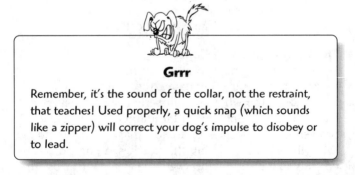

Grrr

Remember, it's the sound of the collar, not the restraint, that teaches! Used properly, a quick snap (which sounds like a zipper) will correct your dog's impulse to disobey or to lead.

Don't be discouraged if you get it wrong a time or two; just keep trying until you've got it right. First, decide which side you want your dog to walk on. As left is traditional, I'll use left as my example:

➤ Take one loop of the collar and slide the slack part of the chain through it.

➤ Pretending you're on *Sesame Street,* make the letter *P* with the chain.

➤ Holding it out with the *P* facing you, stand *in front* of your dog. Show him your creation.

➤ With the *P* still facing you, slide the collar over the dog's head as you praise.

➤ To check the result, slide the rings up behind his ears and stand at his left side. Grasp the moveable ring and pull it toward your leg. Does it slide freely through the stationary loop (you got it!) or does it bend over the stationary loop (try again)?

Sarah Says

If your dog is fussy, give him a biscuit just before you slide the collar across his nose.

If you still find yourself in a constant pulling battle with your dog, only broken by occasional hacking, you might want to investigate other collar options.

To put on a training collar, create the letter P with the chain and slide the collar over your dog's head.

Leashes

There are two types of leashes. One is your six-foot garden variety, made from either cotton, leather, or nylon. The second is a recent invention of mine that received two patents for design and methodology. I call it the *Teaching Lead,* and it's useful in training basics and versatile for everyday use. The difference between the two? One you hold and the other, the Teaching Lead, you wear.

Sound funky? Why would you want to wear a leash? I designed it to communicate leadership passively. Besides that, you can walk through town with your hands free. Pretty cool!

When holding the leash, your hand is everything. Many people curl their fingers under the leash, which is incorrect. It encourages the dog to pull forward and lift up. Instead, hold the leash with your knuckles facing the sky and your thumb wrapped around the underside of the leash. Confused? Here's a little exercise: Hold your left arm straight out from your body. Pointing your thumb downward, lower your arm. As you do, curl your thumb under the lead and wrap your knuckles over the top.

Sarah Says

Whichever leash you use, you must teach your dog that you're the one to watch.

The Magic Seven

Before you go any further, you need to make sure your dog understands the basics. He won't have to win ribbons in a show to move on to the fancy stuff, but he'll need to know seven key commands. I call them the *Magic Seven*:

➤ Name

➤ Name, Let's Go

➤ No Sir (or Ma'am)

➤ Sit and Stay

➤ Wait and Okay (or Stand)

➤ Down

➤ Excuse Me

When I was a kid I remember taking a dog-training class with an instructor who told everyone to practice twice a day for fifteen minutes. Not unusual or bad advice, but who can find the time in this fast-paced world we live in?

I'll tell you what I do now: I use the seven basic commands conversationally throughout the day. "Sit" before petting or treats, "Excuse Me" when a dog's underfoot, "Let's Go" to change direction, and "No" for the naughty stuff. Without taking time out of your day, you can teach your dog the Magic Seven too.

Hand Signals

You can start teaching your dog hand signals as soon as he masters each trick. It's pretty nifty and also encourages better eye contact. I'll suggest one for each new routine. Eventually you'll be able to direct your dog with a slight flick of the wrist. Abracadabra!

Name

Your first goal is to get your dog to alert to his name: "Name," check in. "Name," check in. There are two sure-fire techniques to use.

The first is treat cups. Place some broken-up treats in a plastic cup. Make multiple cups and place them all around your house. Every time you walk by the cup, shake it and call out your dog's name. When he looks to you with all four paws on the floor, say, "Good boy!" and offer him a treat.

The second way to make sure your dog alerts to his name is to take him into a quiet room once a day and, standing tall, call out his name. When your eyes connect, hold your stare until he looks away, then praise him and leave the room. Don't overdo this one. Once a day in a quiet setting is enough.

Hand Signals

Does your dog jump wildly when he hears the cup shake?
If so, look up to the ceiling and don't look down until all
four paws are firmly planted on the floor. Teach everyone
this Four Paw Rule.

Name, Let's Go

After you've got your dog to focus on his name, it's time
to teach him proper following manners. With your dog
on a leash, hold the end loop firmly or secure it around
your waist if you're using the Teaching Lead. Now walk
forward confidently. The second your dog forges ahead
call, "Name, Let's Go" and turn away from him promptly
without thought or encouragement. Continue to do this
until your dog figures out that you're the one to watch.

Sarah Says

Your dog will learn best if you progress from limited
distractions to more stimulating areas.

No Sir (or Ma'am)

This is one of the most important commands your dog
must learn. I know, it's obvious, but most dogs aren't clear
on the true meaning of this word. Some hear "No" so
much that they think it's their name!

To teach your dog to obey No Sir (or Ma'am), you must first teach him the definition. Here's how:

➤ With your dog in the next room, place a plate of cookies on the floor.

➤ Put your dog on a leash and bring him into the room. Approach the plate.

➤ The very second your dog notices the plate, snap the leash back firmly and say "No Sir (or Ma'am)."

➤ Walk by the cookies.

➤ If your dog shows any interest whatsoever, repeat the procedure.

➤ Play this game the next day, with some cheese or steak perhaps.

➤ Keep the corrections focused on the deed. After your dog turns his attention back to you, praise him, and continue your walk.

Pretty soon your dog will see a plate on the floor and turn his nose toward the sky: *"I don't see anything!"*

Sarah Says

There is a strong connection between the leash snap and the No Sir command. The two of them must happen simultaneously for any long-term, off-leash value. The snap alone works, but if you forget to say "No Sir," your dog will have no idea what you're talking about when he's off leash.

Now you're ready to start using No Sir around everyday distractions. Try it with one of your snacks. Keeping your dog on a leash, sit in a chair. Have an Oreo, a potato chip, or perhaps a piece of cheese. If his nose shifts in your direction, snap the leash back and say "No Sir!" Do this without making eye contact.

Sit and Stay

Sit is the first of the stationary commands, and it's necessary to learn in order to get to the fun stuff. Teach it by using this common sense approach: Give the command "Sit" once before anything your dog perceives as positive:

➤ Meals

➤ Treats or toys

➤ Pats

➤ Greeting after an absence

Give the Sit command once, gently positioning your dog if he doesn't listen. Avoid repeating yourself, since repeating isn't cool in any language. After one week, gradually taper off the positive rewards but keep the praise going.

Hand Signals

Use hand signals with your commands from the start. For sit, swing your open right hand from your dog's nose to your eyes, as if you're scooping his attention toward you.

Next, introduce the Stay command. At first, say it while standing at your dog's side: "Stay," then pause–2–3, and release with "Okay!" Now tell your dog to "Stay" and pivot directly in front of him. Return to his side and release with "Okay!" As your dog catches on, increase your distance and add some distractions (you can hop around or make funny sounds—it'll be fun).

Wait and Okay

The second stationary command, Wait and Okay, is a real prize. It means to stand still and wait to be released. First you must teach the dog that Wait means stop, stand, and focus; then he learns Okay means it's all right to move. It's permission training, step two. It's a self-control thing. You teach it like this:

➤ Pick any threshold in your home.

➤ Holding your dog to your side on leash, walk to this threshold.

➤ Stop abruptly as you reach the threshold and say "Wait."

➤ If he bolts anyway, pull him back behind your heels and repeat "Wait!"

➤ Repeat the pullback as often as necessary until he pauses and looks to you.

➤ After he's checked in, say "Okay" and lead him through.

Hand Signals

A flat palm flashed quickly in front of your dog's nose is the hand signal for Wait, and an upbeat flash outward is used for Okay.

Now you're ready for the big time! Go to your main doorway. Prepare yourself as previously, holding the leash behind your body. Command "Wait" just before you open the door. If your dog bolts, be ready. Snap him back behind your feet and repeat "Wait." When he does, say "Okay" as you lead him through.

After you've mastered the front door, try the car. Take your dog to your car and instruct him to "Wait" as you open the door. If he lunges, snap him back, refusing to let him in until he looks to you for permission.

Down

The last of our stationary commands, Down, is a beauty. So applicable and so useful. Initially this exercise can be a real bear to teach, but if you build it around positives your dog will catch on in no time.

- ➤ Take out a favorite toy or treat.

- ➤ Give the command "Sit," then take the treat and hold it on the ground slightly in front of him.

- ➤ Let your dog puzzle over the predicament, but don't release the prize or say anything until his elbows touch the floor.

- ➤ As he lowers himself, say "Down," then praise, reward, and release him.

Continue this exchange for anything positive. After three days, say "Down" from a standing position, adding your hand signal, which is a downward drop of your left hand. Continue the reward exchange for another three days, then begin to phase out the object reward, relying solely on your verbal praise.

Excuse Me

This command must be said with an ounce of attitude. It's a good one when your dog is underfoot, crosses in front of you, or swings to the wrong side when you're walking.

What's the point, you ask? Well in dogland, subordinates watch out for their leaders. So to answer your question, Excuse Me communicates leadership; it demands respect. So now a question for you: How often does your dog naturally watch out for you? How often does he automatically get up and move aside when you pass? Are some of you laughing? You're not alone.

Grrr

A dog must learn the *three-inch exclusion zone.* Unless invited in, he must respect this space between you and him. Crowding is a sign of dominance or insecurity; neither is good for long-term relationships.

New rules, however. If your dog is in your way, say "Excuse Me" and move him to one side. No stepping over. No walking around. No changing direction. If he won't move, shimmy your feet beneath him or nudge him aside with your knees. Don't renavigate an inch.

Chapter 2

Whatever Makes Their Tails Wag

The Building Block Approach

When teaching fun and useful tricks, keep your training sessions short and sweet; no more than five minutes. Repeat the sessions one to four times during the day. Your dog *will* learn, as long as you're positive and use the *building block approach*.

"What's the building block approach?" you ask. It's fairly simple. Each new routine will have steps to follow, and you need to perfect each step before moving onto the next. Let's look at jumping through a hoop. The first step is to get your dog to jump over a low broom when he hears the command Over. The next step is to let him get accustomed to the hoop at ground level; as he walks through, he should hear the command Through.

Step three is to put the two together by holding the hoop above the broom, and step four is to ask your dog to jump through the hoop alone. So we have four steps. Because your dog can't master an entire routine in five minutes, you'll need to isolate each step and build on your dog's successes. There we have it folks . . . the building block approach.

Sarah Says

The first time your dog perfects a routine, offer him a *jackpot* and a load of praise. Jackpots are a special treat or toy, or a handful of the rewards you use for training, to let your dog know how psyched you are that he got it!

When Praise Alone Won't Do

You might be lucky enough to have the rare dog that responds to your desires just to make you happy. "You want me to fetch you a soda instead of resting here by this sunny window? Where's the fridge?" Then again, you might not.

I'm sure many of my clients are reading this with their jaw on the floor, recalling my classroom lectures about the mortal sins of using treats with training. That rule still counts with Obedience work (where food is forbidden in the competition ring), but trick training is another matter. The word "trick" itself conjures up visions of magic, laughter, and fun, and while you're enjoying the fruits of your training, your dog shouldn't be left out.

What you'll use to entice your dog will depend on your dog. First you must decide exactly what makes his tail wag hardest. Is it food? Toys? You?

Food

Does your dog live for food? He's in the majority. Now you'll need to figure out what your dog likes best. Strive for low-cal rewards that are easy and quick to swallow. Whenever possible, I use Cheerios (the breakfast cereal). If your dog turns up his nose, however, you'll need to find something a bit more tempting.

Most dogs would fly like a rocket for dried hotdog bits. To see what yours thinks, cut a slice off a hotdog and nuke it in the microwave for sixty seconds. After letting it cool, offer it up. Yes? If not, you'll have to continue your search.

Whatever food you end up with, cut it into small pieces so that when you're training, he won't fill up.

Grrr

Treats should be small and easy to swallow so your dog won't take too long or fill up. Don't treat your dog when he's not having lessons, or it won't seem as exciting.

Toys

Have you ever seen a dog that lives for a toy? It's quite remarkable—like a child and a security blanket. If this is your pal, your job is easy. To encourage responsiveness, all you'll need to do is control the toy. Get your dog accustomed to hearing a phrase like, "Where's your ball?" or "Get your toy!" so that you can use it to reinforce his efforts.

Now that you've discovered what really revs your dog's engine, use it. As he improves, he'll respond just for the fun of it, but for the learning process you'll have to egg him on with whatever makes his tail wag!

Clicker Training

I was first introduced to clickers at a three-day seminar in Phoenix, Arizona. Apparently I was late on the scene, so if you don't know what a clicker is, don't feel bad. In technical terms a *clicker* is a small handheld device that is used to "mark" behaviors when they occur. In everyday English, it's a small box that you use to make a distinct clicking sound at the same time you hand out your dog's favorite reward. Each time he does what you want him to do, you can let him know quickly and clearly. Am I confusing you? Let's take a closer look.

A clicker

When you press the metal strip inside a clicker, it lets out a distinct click, which is quickly followed by a treat or toy. For example, if you were teaching your dog to kiss, you would click the second he gave a kiss, then quickly offer his favorite reward. Timing is everything with the clicker, because your dog will know the sound soon after you introduce him to it. Here's how to get started:

➤ Buy a clicker.

➤ Line up your dog's favorite treats or toys on a table.

➤ Click and offer the treat or toy and praise.

➤ Repeat this 10 times; click and reward (saying "Good dog!" too).

➤ After your dog connects the click with the reward, you're ready to use the clicker to teach your first trick.

Sarah Says

Using clickers is optional. It's one *very* fun way to teach tricks, but you can also snap your fingers, make a clicking sound with your tongue, or use a sharp, happy word like "Yes!" to let your dog know he's on the right track.

Touch This, Touch That

After your dog understands the clicker-reward connection, take a long object such as the end of a kitchen utensil or a pencil tip and hold it out for your dog. The second he touches it with his nose, click and reward. Don't say anything yet; just click and reward until your dog makes the connection.

When your dog figures out that all he has to do to get the treat is to touch the end of the object, begin to introduce the command Touch. Using the same object, hold it to your dog's left and his right. Hold it in front and in back. Up and down. Move it around little by little until your dog follows the pointer like a magnet, gently touching it each time. We'll be using this routine as a building block to many others, so congratulate yourselves—you've just performed your first trick!

Grrr

If your dog mouths the paper or the pointer, try practicing with him at a low-energy time and use the No Sir command learned in the previous chapter. Don't introduce too much discipline, however, or your dog won't want to work with you. Click only for responses where your dog's mouth is shut! Selectively rewarding will do the job without disciplining.

With clicker training, getting everything in the right order is important. So it's worth repeating. When teaching your dog with the clicker, keep this sequence in mind:

➤ Click and reward the instant your dog does what you want.

➤ After your dog makes the connection and starts responding voluntarily, introduce a command.

➤ Have your dog repeat the behavior a few times before the click, and reward.

➤ When your dog listens to the command, taper off the use of the clicker.

Stand Here, Stand There

Another essential foundation is to have your dog stand in a specified spot. This trick requires more patience, but once learned it's never forgotten. Here's how to teach it:

➤ Take a blank sheet of regular typing paper and place it near you on the floor. With clicker and treats ready, sit tight until your dog puts his two front paws on the paper. Click, praise, and reward.

➤ Pick up the paper, move it a few inches and wait again. You may have to wait a while in the beginning, so be patient. When your dog's front paws hit the paper, click, praise, and reward.

➤ In the beginning it won't matter which direction your dog's facing or what position he's in when his front paws hit the paper. But after he gets the idea, start clicking only when your dog is facing you.

➤ After your dog catches on, you can start saying the command "Here" and just pointing to the paper. Click, reward, and praise!

➤ When your dog is responding to your command, move the paper away from you incrementally.

➤ Now go back to the first step (close by your feet), but use a smaller piece of paper, perhaps cutting a few inches off the original.

➤ Your goal is to be able to send your dog across the room to stand on a small business card and give him his trick commands at a distance. This is the long-range plan.

Chapter 3

A Go-Active Health Plan

In This Chapter

➤ Starting out with a clean bill of health

➤ How to get your dog into a healthy routine at home

➤ The importance of conditioning (for both of you!)

➤ Recognizing your dog's physical potential

Because many of the activities in this book require physical exertion, your dog needs a health clearance from your veterinarian. Dogs, being dogs, will do their best to please you, even when they're not feeling well. You need to recognize problems and be sensitive when your dog is under the weather. Also, for those sworn couch potatoes, you'll need to start with some proper conditioning before you set your sights on the Broadway lights or sign up to run the Iditarod!

A Clean Bill of Health

What exactly does clean bill of health mean? For the right answer, I went to a pro: my veterinarian.

Your Veterinarian's Approval

My veterinarian started out with a checklist:

➤ **Pulse.** A dog's pulse should be between 60 and 160 beats per minute at rest, depending on his size; smaller dog, faster pulse. A quick listen with a stethoscope (no talking please) will tell if the blood's flowing properly.

➤ **Breathing.** Breathing is one of life's simple pleasures. It's essential for all living things. Your veterinarian will listen to make sure your dog inhales and exhales properly.

➤ **Coat and skin.** Different breeds have different coats. My vet likes to see a coat that's free from parasites and properly oiled. When checking the skin, it's important that it be clear and smooth. Any lumps, loss of hair, discoloration, scales, or pimples are cause for alarm.

➤ **Eyes.** A dog's eyes should be free of mucus and hair and not too pink. A glance under the third eyelid will tell if a dog's in good health or if there's an infection or sickness elsewhere in the body.

➤ **Ears.** A dog's ear has a big flap that makes it more likely than ours to gather dirt and moisture—which can cause an infection. Your veterinarian will check the ears to make sure they're clean and that your dog can hear what you're saying.

➤ **Teeth.** It's a good idea to brush your dog's teeth. My vet provides me with a kit. He even insisted on one for my cat! An examination of your dog's mouth will tell if his gums are infected or if he's suffering from periodontal disease.

➤ **Paw pads and nails.** A dog's paw pads should be soft, not rough. Avoid wear and tear on concrete or pebbled surfaces and keep your dog clear of broken glass. Your veterinarian will check his nails and cut them if they are too long. Overgrown nails are uncomfortable.

➤ **Bones and tissues.** A proper check-up should include rotation of the major joints to make sure your dog's skeleton is aligned or your puppy's growth plates are developing normally.

➤ **Vaccines.** Your veterinarian also will notify you of your dog's vaccine schedule. Vaccines are given first during puppyhood and are continued throughout a dog's life.

➤ **A sample, please.** The final things your veterinarian will want to check are your dog's stool, urine, and blood to make sure nothing alien is floating inside. Bring in a stool sample and don't let your dog pee until after his exam!

Home Care

Now that you've got your veterinarian's blessing, it's time to set up a home clinic to keep your dog in shape. Brushes, nail clippers, toothpaste, cotton swabs, monthly medications . . . these are just some of the paraphernalia you'll use to keep your dog in top condition.

Brushing

Grooming can be your worst nightmare or your best friend. If the thought of brushing your dog troubles you, try this:

➤ Start with a soft-bristled brush.

➤ Call your dog aside happily, giving him a treat when he comes.

➤ Take some peanut butter and rub it on a wall at your dog's nose level.

➤ While he licks it off, say "Stand" and brush gently. Praise too!

➤ Quit while you're ahead and increase the brushing time slowly. Eventually, your dog will consider brush times endearing.

Bathing

Everyone has to bathe their dog. To make it a positive experience, lay a towel on the bottom of the sink or tub (for your dog to stand on comfortably without slipping) and spread peanut butter around the edge to occupy your dog while you scrub.

Grrr

Dogs should only be bathed once a month. Shampooed too often, their coat will dry out and become brittle.

My Nails, Darling

Unfortunately, dogs don't relate to the whole manicure thing the way some women do. I hate to sound redundant, but using treats or peanut butter can calm the most savage beast!

The best nail clipper looks like a guillotine. When clipping, make sure you clip the very tip of the nail, just as it starts to curl. (If your dog has light-colored nails, you can see the delicate blood vessel inside; that's the part you want to avoid!) And don't overlook dew claws or hind nails. Though they grow more slowly, they still need your attention. If nails grow too long they can crack, break, or become ingrown. Ouch!

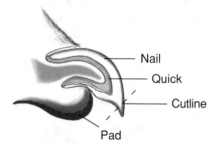

Nail
Quick
Cutline
Pad

Cut on the dotted line.

If your dog's not comfortable having her feet handled, make it a part of your everyday interactions. Handle the feet when giving a treat, petting, or feeding. Tell your dog how wonderful her feet are. Kiss them when she's sleeping. (Okay, you don't *have to* kiss your dog's feet, but you can.)

If your dog is totally opposed to the clipper, you'll have to do some conditioning work there, too. Let your dog get accustomed to the sound when you're playing or talking to her. Then clip around your dog's paws, without coming into contact. Next, try cutting one nail—just one. Slowly build up her tolerance, one nail at a time!

Grrr

God forbid you cut into your dog's tissue! Aside from it being excruciatingly painful, it can bleed for hours. To prevent excess bleeding, get a clotting solution from your veterinarian. It works like magic. In a pinch, a little bit of cornstarch will fill in—but the clotting solution is better.

Look at That Face

Dogs don't spend as much time on their looks as you do, but that doesn't mean their facial features should go unnoticed.

Eyes

Soulful, sweet, comic—your dog's eyes tell it all. It's up to you to keep the eyes healthy, bright, and clear. Don't let your dog hang her head out of the car window. Sure, it looks refreshing, but one pebble could knock out an eye for good!

Also, be careful when playing games or practicing tricks that call for the use of a pointy object or stick. Eyes are very tender! Take care of them and take your dog to the doctor if his eyes get tearful, red, swollen, or itchy.

If your veterinarian prescribes eye medication, administer it carefully. Use peanut butter on the fridge or a bowl of broth in a friend's lap to occupy your dog while you medicate him. Place your hand carefully under your dog's chin and pull the lower eyelid down until you see the white part. Squeeze the drops in there.

Sarah Says

If you have a longhaired breed, carefully clip the hair surrounding the eyes. Better to see you with!

Ears

I'm mesmerized by this body part. I can lull myself into a trance petting ears and it doesn't seem to matter what shape—uprights, floppy, short, or cropped. Dogs seem to love the ear massage, too.

Different dogs require different cleaning schedules, from every couple of weeks to daily. Your dog's activity and the weather also influence the frequency of cleaning. If your dog is an Olympic swimmer, I suggest daily cleaning before bed. In most cases, twice a month is sufficient.

Grrr

Never, never, never use a Q-tip or poke your finger into your dog's ear. You can do irreparable damage!

To clean the outer flap, ask your veterinarian to recommend a commercial ear solution that will prevent infection. Soak a cotton swab with the solution and wipe the outer earflap.

If your dog's ear gets infected, follow the same procedure that was used for medicating the eye. If your dog has drop ears, gently lift the flap and place the medicine where your veterinarian has instructed.

Nose

There's not too much to say about the dog's nose. When I was growing up, people used to say you could tell a dog's mood by touching his nose. If it was hot, the dog was sick; too dry, the dog was depressed. The truth is there's no truth to those old wives' tales. A dog's nose can heat up in a warm environment and can dry out when the air is dry. If you want to know if your dog's running a fever, take his temperature—rectal style!

A dog's nose can get discolored. How? Sometimes from the sun or other times it can be an allergic reaction to a food dish or household detergent. In such a case, use a stainless steel bowl and clean with environmentally safe products. And when your dog goes out into the sun, protect that nose with sunblock SPF 45!

Mouth

I have one obsession: It's my teeth. I love brushing, flossing, and going to the dentist. Odd, I know. Based on this, you probably know what I'm going to suggest before I even write it. You must take care of your dog's teeth. Though dogs are less prone to tartar build-up than you are, they're not immune. Sure, they have more-concentrated saliva and they chew bones and things, but this doesn't take the place of dental care. Without a little help from their friends (that's you), they'll suffer from tooth decay, cavities, abscesses, periodontal disease, and tooth loss.

To keep your dog's teeth healthy:

➤ Feed dry food. Crunchy is better.

➤ Brush your dog's teeth once a week, using special canine toothpaste. If your dog won't settle for the brush, use your finger.

Grrr

Avoid human toothpaste; fluoride and dogs don't mix.

Conditioning, Conditioning

Now that you can rest assured your dog is healthy, you need to make sure he's in top physical condition, or has a program to get him there, before you jump into this new activity regime. Just like humans, pushing your dog too far too fast can lead to trouble.

The Hip Bone's Connected to the Thigh Bone

If you took a look inside your little trickster, you'd see that you're a lot alike. Sure the bones are stacked differently, but they're all there, put together as perfectly as a puzzle. And like us, dogs' bones are glued together with special tissues called ligaments. The place where bones meet each other is called a joint, and its movement and flexibility are controlled by tendons, which connect muscle to bone. Where free-moving joints meet, the ends are protected by a layer of cartilage.

In a perfect world this puzzle would always be the same, but there is no such thing as a perfect world. Each dog in the world has a unique conformation, and understanding your dog's physical strengths and limitations is necessary for training.

Physicalities

If your dog's anything like me, the thought of exercising will send him flying under the covers. Fortunately, however, most dogs aren't like me. They love to run and play and be a part of whatever you're doing. If your dog has not been out for a good run in a long time, you'll need to ease him in slowly. Conditioning for dogs is like conditioning for us—a necessary evil.

Start with conditioning for tricks and obedience. Most of the stunts outlined in this book don't require tremendous amounts of physical exertion. However, if your dog has been off the training wagon for some time, keep the lessons short and upbeat to start: No more than three minutes. He doesn't have to master a trick a day.

Start with tricks that are easy for him to master and that make you laugh. Laughter is great encouragement. You can have practice sessions three times a day if your schedule allows, but short lessons are best.

Conditioning for activities is another thing. Are you pumped up to start racing that dog of yours over every tree and up ladders? Whoa Nellie! Your dog will want to try everything you introduce him to, but is he ready? If your dog can't tell a tree stump from an ottoman, start small. No need to conquer the world in a day.

First, take a couple of weeks to make sure your dog can handle the excitement. Go for half-mile hikes, building the distance over time. A four-month-old pup will run until his legs can't carry him, but all that exercise can permanently alter his growing muscles and cause hip problems later in life. I know—teaching your dog new stuff is a lot of fun, but you need to be the parent here and do what is best for your dog.

Grrr

Do not jump your puppy higher than the height of his elbow. Also avoid over-feeding your pup. Extra weight can strain developing growth plates!

Never forget the age factor. Growing pups are in the majority where sports injuries are concerned. A young dog's energy and enthusiasm can be quite misleading: They'll want to try everything and give no thought to the consequences. Trauma to bones and joints is caused by overstrenuous activity, slippery footing, or excessive jumping. During your puppy's growth phase—four-and-a-half to nine months—keep his activity level regulated and do not encourage jumping.

Let's talk breeds. Picture a Dachshund: dwarfed-out legs, long body, endearing eyes, and the greatest paddle paws on the planet. Now clear your head and envision a Boxer: upright, statuesque, proud, magnificently angled, and proportioned to a T. No one on the planet would ever ask them both for the same performance.

Make sure you monitor the activity level of growing puppies.

One has legs meant for digging, the other for running. Now go take a look at your dog. What breed or mix of breeds have you got? Sure you may be all hyped for Agility trials, but if your Bulldog Mugs is snoring on the couch, don't plan on taking home any trophies.

Chapter 4

Sports Injuries

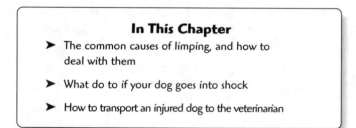

In This Chapter

➤ The common causes of limping, and how to deal with them

➤ What do to if your dog goes into shock

➤ How to transport an injured dog to the veterinarian

Activity training, whether it be the simplest tricks, such as wagging the tail, or jumping an Agility wall, requires movement. And with all movement there is the possibility of injury. From a torn ligament or cartilage to a slipped spinal disc, you must learn to read your dog's signs because he can't talk to you.

If your dog has an accident during a workout, you need to stay cool. If you lose it, he'll get nervous and go to pieces. Be a rock of confidence. Be mentally tough. Organize. Think. If need be, get him to the hospital as quickly and carefully as possible.

Let's take a look at some of the things that can happen to your active dog, what causes them, and how to cope.

Limping

This is the most common result of a sports injury. Your job is to find out what is causing your dog to limp and which body part is in trouble. To figure out just where the pain is centralized:

➤ Watch your dog. When he's standing still it should be obvious which leg is being favored.

➤ Now watch him walk. He'll take a shorter step on his injured leg. His head also may bob up and down to compensate for the pressure he's trying to keep off his hurt limb.

➤ To pinpoint the specific injury site, carefully rub your hands along your dog's joints and note any muscle tenderness.

➤ If you're still puzzled, gently flex and rotate your dog's joints.

➤ Now check for discoloration and swelling and take your dog's temperature with a rectal thermometer. (Oh joy!)

Remember that the quicker an injury is diagnosed, the easier it is to treat and the less likely it is your dog will need surgery. That's why it's important to see your veterinarian whenever your dog gets hurt.

Genetic Skeletal Disorders

Genetic disorders are passed from parent dogs to puppies on blueprints known as genes. Hip dysplasia, which mostly occurs in larger dogs, both pure-bred and mixed, is one of these genetic disorders. Normally, the head of the

Limping is the most common result of a sports injury.

femur (thigh bone) fits into the hip socket and rotates freely as your dog moves around. In a perfect world it would always be so. In a moderately dysplastic dog, however, loose ligaments allow the head of the femur to begin to work free. A shallow cup in the hip socket also contributes to this condition.

Because of this joint laxity, there is abnormal wear and tear on the joint. In time this leads to arthritis in the dysplastic joint.

Mild dysplasia creates slips in motion, discomfort, and instability. When hip dysplasia is severe, it's extremely painful. The X-rays make you cringe. With the femoral head degenerated and practically dislocated, motion is crippled and pain is constant. Your veterinarian will inform you of surgical options.

If your dog has a skeletal disorder such as hip or elbow dysplasia, I'm sorry. It's a big disappointment for both of you, but what are you going to do? You must deal with it and respect the limitations it will put on training. First, a checklist of things you can do:

✓ Neuter your dog. Don't pass on your dog's problem to future generations.

✓ Feed your dog a balanced diet.

✓ Avoid high calorie, rapid-growth diets. They can aggravate the disorder. The tissues, bones, and muscles must grow together evenly.

✓ Avoid supplementing the diet, especially with calcium. Ask for your veterinarian's suggestion.

✓ Keep your dog's weight down. Too many pounds on a stressed joint is a bad thing.

✓ Talk to your dog's breeder. They should know of your heartache. If they're responsible, they'll eliminate that breeding combination.

✓ Avoid all contributing environmental factors. Long jogs are no good. Correct jumping habits. Are stairs stressful? Talk to your veterinarian.

✓ Buy cozy bedding. Heating pads too . . . ah, heaven!

✓ Carpet any area your dog travels frequently. Slippery floors don't provide good traction.

✓ Avoid leaving your dog out in the cold. Keep him in a warm, dry environment, especially at night.

✓ Last, but not least, massage that joint. (Avoid putting pressure on the joint itself.) Get blood flowing to the muscles, especially if your dog is on bed rest.

There is a wonderful exercise for dysplastic dogs: swimming. Not everyone is fortunate to have a pond or pool in the backyard, but if you look hard enough you may be able to find a place nearby where your dog can swim. Long swims and leash walks on turf (no cement) can build the muscles up and slowly build your dog's strength.

If you have a setback and the limping starts again, talk to your veterinarian and ease off strenuous exercise and training. Start back slowly when you're given the go-ahead. Your dog is physically handicapped. He needs you to take care of him.

Shock

A dog can go into shock if there's a sudden loss of blood, a trauma, or electrocution. Shock is life threatening; it causes blood pressure to drop dramatically, which prevents oxygen from circulating in the body. Without oxygen, the body dies quickly.

A dog in shock shows the following symptoms:

➤ A fast heart rate, as the heart tries to make up for a drop in blood pressure

➤ Rapid breathing, because the body is trying to increase oxygen flow

➤ Dilated pupils and a glaring stare

➤ Unconscious or semiconscious behavior

If you suspect your dog has gone into shock, stay calm, keep him still, and get to the nearest veterinarian immediately.

Transporting an Injured Dog

Transporting a dog who has internal injuries is tricky business. They'll be restless and want to move, and it's your job to make sure they don't. It's best to have someone help you out, so they can drive and you can comfort and restrain your dog. If someone isn't available immediately, however, don't delay in getting your dog to the vet.

Sarah Says

Be ready! Place towels and a dog-sized board aside for emergencies.

If you suspect a broken bone, spinal injury, or internal bleeding, transport your dog on a firm surface such as metal or plywood. Otherwise, placing your dog on a sheet or towel is acceptable. Don't cover his face, as it may completely freak him out.

Chapter 5

Diet: A Dog's Eye View

In This Chapter

➤ Proteins, carbohydrates, and fats, oh my!

➤ What is that stuff in dog food?

➤ Dry food vs. wet

➤ What's right for Fido isn't right for Rover

There is more to a fun-loving, happy dog than interaction and training. You need to learn about keeping your dog healthy and well-balanced on the inside, and it starts with a good diet.

I have to admit I was fairly ignorant about dog foods before I started working as a dog trainer. "A little of this, a little of that" was the stated dog food in my house while growing up. Poor Shawbee, my childhood dog, had a lot of gas to contend with from her irregular fare. Over the years I've learned a lot about dog nutrition. And I'll tell you, it's been a major revelation.

What's in Dog Food?

A good diet is like setting a sturdy foundation before you start building your house. If you don't do it, you could have the finest training regime in history, but your dog won't live up to his fullest potential.

All dog foods aren't the same. Like books and people, you can't judge the contents by what you see on the cover. To pick the right food you'll need to consider (who else?) your dog: his age, breed, and lifestyle.

Dog foods do have certain things in common. To pass regulatory standards, they must contain six essential elements: protein, fat, carbohydrates, vitamins, minerals, and water. But that's where the similarities usually end. The makers of dog foods diverge on what ingredients are used to reach the minimum daily requirement (MDR). For example, some use soy (a vegetable protein) to meet the daily protein requirement, while others use animal protein. Let's look at the essentials one at a time.

Sarah Says

As you learn about dog foods and check out a variety of brands, you'll discover that foods that cost more aren't always best.

Protein

Protein is the most expensive ingredient in dog foods. Its source often determines the quality of the food. Animal sources are superior. Unfortunately, there's not enough meat around to satisfy all the pet dogs in the world, so we have come up with substitute food: vegetable protein. The difference between vegetable and animal protein? Vegetable is often harder to digest and more of it has to be consumed to meet the dog's needs. More food equals more stool. The moral of the story is: Find a food that uses more animal protein and requires smaller rations to meet the MDR.

Grrrr

More protein is not always better. High protein diets are used for show or working dogs. If your dog's mellow or spends many hours alone, feeding a high-protein diet will make her jittery and hyper.

Carbohydrates

Some manufacturers meet the MDR for protein by using primarily vegetable matter. Vegetable sources of protein also contain high levels of carbohydrates; not a bad diet for humans, but what's good for humans isn't always good for dogs. The reason we digest carbohydrates well is that we start digestion in our mouths, chewing and breaking down the food as it goes. Dogs don't chew, they gulp, and their digestion doesn't begin until the food gets into their stomach.

Why is this important? Foods high in carbs can cause digestive problems in dogs, such as bloating, upset stomach, constipation, and too much stool. Make sure you pick a diet that contains more animal protein than vegetable protein. How? Read the label and select a food that has two or more animal sources of protein listed in the first five ingredients.

Fats

Please don't ever buy fat-free dog food. I know it sounds tempting, but your dog needs fat to keep her skin and coat healthy and to transport things around on the inside. Used in the proper moderation, fat will give your dog energy and keep her cool when it's warm and warm when it's cool.

However, fat can be a funny thing. For one, it spoils quickly. If you're feeding your dog a natural diet make sure you respect the expiration date. Rancid fat can lead to a whole slew of health problems.

Vitamins and Minerals

Have you ever wondered what vitamins exactly do and why they're necessary for good health? Vitamins do two things:

➤ They unlock nutrients from food.

➤ They provide energy.

The need for vitamins varies depending on your dog and his lifestyle. The average bag of dog food, however, doesn't take this into consideration. The truth is the MDR was set for laboratory Beagle-type dogs. Take that into account, along with the fact that vitamins are a rather unstable lot, easily destroyed by light and heat, and you'd be wise to invest in a good vitamin supplement. Ask your veterinarian for a suggestion.

Vitamin deficiencies can lead to poor growth, digestive disorders, elimination problems, stool eating, a weak

immune system, greasy and stinky coats, Addison's
Disease (thyroid malfunction), aggression, timidity, and
sterility. Not a pretty list!

Minerals are a lot like their cohorts vitamins. They help
the body maintain its normal daily activities, such as
circulation, energy production, and cell regeneration.
Although mineral deficiencies are not that uncommon,
do not supplement your dog's diet unless directed by
your veterinarian. That's because too many minerals can
cause health problems.

Water

Did you know that your dog can live three weeks
without food, but will die within days without water?
Water is necessary for all digestive processes as well as
temperature regulation, nutrient absorption, and as a
transportation medium, shipping things between organs
and out of the body.

How much water your dog will need depends on his
physical activities and the type of food he eats. Panting
is your dog's way of sweating. If your dog is panting, he
needs a drink. Dry food also encourages thirst. On the
other hand, canned food or home-cooked diets contain
more water and require less to rinse and wash down.

Choosing Your Dog's Diet

Deciding on a diet for your dog is no small order.
Commercial, dry, canned, home-cooked; the choice is
yours, and it isn't an easy one. Every diet doesn't suit
every dog, so be a conscientious shopper. Let's take a
look at each option.

Commercial Foods

Here are four constants to help you make your selection:

> ➤ Look for the AAFCO (American Association of Feed
>   Control Officials) stamp of approval.

> ➤ Note the suggested daily ration. Is it realistic?

> ➤ Eliminate foods causing weight loss; loose, smelly
>   stools; or poor coat condition.

> ➤ Respect your dog's judgment. Refusal to touch the
>   food can be attributed to stubbornness, but it's often
>   a sign of spoiled ingredients or allergies.

Next, consider your lifestyle. Do you have a lot of free
time to train your dog and engage in high-energy
activities? Performance foods with high levels of crude
protein provide lots of energy to burn. Puppies also need
higher amounts of protein for their growing bodies.

Homemade Diets

There are many pros to a homemade diet for your dog.
Followed responsibly, the home diet can be modified for
your dog's age, breed distinctions, and individual needs.
Personalized diets will enhance your dog's health and
vitality.

The drawbacks? These diets can't be fudged. You must
commit to preparing balanced meals and to shop for
products regularly to ensure freshness. If you want to try
a homemade diet, please refer to *The Holistic Guide for a
Healthy Dog* by Wendy Volhard and Kerry Brown, DVM,
or *Natural Food Recipes for Healthy Dogs* by Carol Boyle
(both from Howell Book House, New York).

Sarah Says

If you want to give your dear dog a bone, please avoid poultry or pork, as they splinter and can have fatal consequences. Beef knuckles and marrow bones are best; just ask your butcher. Parboil them in meat broth to enhance their flavor and kill parasites.

Dry vs. Wet Food

What are the differences between dry food and wet food? Cost in shipping and cost to the consumer. Wet food contains 65 percent to 78 percent water; the weight of the can and water increases the cost of shipping.

Wet food is less likely to fill up your dog with grain fillers that he can't really use anyway. Dry food is better for his teeth. No studies have proven either wet or dry to be nutritionally superior. So what it boils down to is that the choice is up to you. Many of the veterinarians I've talked to suggest a combination of the two.

When searching for the right diet, pay close attention to your dog. How is his digestion? Foods with low-quality ingredients aren't absorbed well and can give your dog loose stools.

Growing Puppies

I'm a sucker for a young puppy, and though I spoil them as much as possible with kisses and head scratches, I never fudge on their diet. Like a human baby, their digestive systems are very fragile. After weaning they should be kept on the same puppy food for at least eight weeks. If you decide to switch brands of food, do it incrementally over a ten-day period.

There are some key differences between people's diets and puppies' diets. Number one, dogs don't dig fiber. A high-fiber, low-fat diet for a dog of any age could be disastrous. Stool city. Remember dogs are born carnivores, and no New Age fad will change that! Monitor protein and calories if you want to raise a healthy pup. They need more of both, as they're growing mentally and physically.

Grrr

Overfeeding or sprinkling your puppy's diet with table scraps is a bad thing. Puppies who obsess over food and mealtimes are likely to become pudgy and fat. This is bad for the growth of their bones and muscles and is likely to cause development problems down the road.

How much food your puppy will eat depends on his size and weight. Often the portions listed on the back of the bag are exaggerated or estimated for an average dog. And who has an average dog? Not you! To decide on the right amount of food, ask your puppy. Give him as much he'll eat in fifteen minutes and then feed him that much at each meal. If he eats it all, don't offer more. If he doesn't eat anything, don't fret. Dogs are just like that.

How often you feed your puppy will depend on his age and your time schedule. I like to feed a young pup (one that's under twelve weeks) four times a day: 7 A.M., 12 noon, 4 P.M., and 10 P.M. I know, I know . . . lots of stool, lots of stool. But this is how I am.

After twelve weeks I phase out the late-night feeding and continue three meals a day until my puppy stops eating one of those meals or reaches six months (whichever comes first). At this point I can rest assured that my pup's stomach can retain the food for longer periods of time. Adapt your schedule to your puppy's needs.

Overweight Dogs

Putting on extra pounds can happen at any time in a dog's life, although it most often occurs in old age. Metabolism slows, and so does the interest in exercising. Fortunately, we live in an age of low-cal dog food that is perfectly balanced for the sedentary dog.

Sarah Says

Here's a quick check to see if your dog's got one too many layers. Stand him up and feel his ribs. If you're having trouble finding them, it's time for a diet!

Add a healthy walk or two daily, and your dog will be swinging those hips around the neighborhood in no time!

Chapter 6

Fun and Simple Tricks

In This Chapter

➤ The classic Paw trick, with six variations

➤ Playing dog-style soccer

➤ Teaching Hide and Seek and Catch Me, the great energy burners

---

Remember in high school when you showed up in class to discover that instead of a lecture it was a film day? Your brain let out a big sigh of relief because it knew the hard work was over for the day. Well brain, you can let out a sigh; the tricks and games in this chapter are easy to master. Some games are designed to burn energy and are good to play when your dog is full of beans. Other tricks are just for fun, and when your dog catches on he'll want to practice as much as you.

Sarah Says

When teaching tricks, speak clearly, directing your words to your dog, and give each command only once.

The Classic Paw, with Variations

Nothing like starting with a classic. Some dogs are naturally predisposed to this action—so much so that you're probably wondering how to teach No Paw, but we'll get to that later.

After you've mastered the Paw, you can really start being creative. For those of you new to this, get your dog (on a leash if he's antsy) some favorite treats and go into a quiet room.

➤ Kneel or sit in front of your dog.

➤ Command Sit. Position if necessary, and praise.

➤ Using a thumb, press your dog's shoulder muscle gently until his front leg lifts.

➤ Shake his paw warmly, then treat and praise.

➤ After you've got the hang of it and his leg lifts easily, start using the command Paw and giving him the hand signal before pressing his muscle (if you still need to).

Hand Signals

Stretch out your hand to the specified paw.

Say Thank You

This is a real charmer. And after your dog learns the signal, performing this trick is a piece of cake. Give the command "Say Thank You" as you extend your hand to your dog with the palm up. Praise and give him a treat. Now get a human pal to help you out. As your friend extends a hand and says "Say Thank You," encourage your dog to offer his paw to your friend. Now you're ready to spread your dog's good manners everywhere!

Other One

As your dog catches on, you'll notice that he favors either his left or right paw. To prevent having a one-dimensional dog, teach him "Other One."

> ➤ Ask "Paw" and lovingly praise your dog.

> ➤ Now extend your hand to the other paw and say, "Other One."

> ➤ If your dog lifts his favored paw, use a sound such as "Ep, Ep" and repeat your original request while you put pressure on the muscle of the other paw.

> ➤ When your dog lifts the other paw, praise, treat, and give him a big hug!

Left Paw, Right Paw

By using Other One to get your dog to pay attention to which hand you extend, you can pull off a trick that makes it seem as if your dog can tell his right paw from his left, the little genius!

While in a quiet room, decide which paw your dog gives most frequently; here we'll say it's the left paw. Exaggerate the hand signal as you hold your hand to his left side and say, "Left Paw." Praise and offer a treat. Do three lefts, so your dog gets plenty of good reinforcement. If by chance your dog swaps and offers a right paw, say, "Ep, ep, ep, not yet" and wait to reward until the left paw is offered.

Now for the other paw. Exaggerate your hand signal toward the right side and say "Right Paw." Your dog will probably try the left paw. If he does, say "Ep, ep, Other One." Show him physically if you have to. Practice three rights, then quit for now.

The next time you go to practice, start with Right Paw, accentuating your signal. Help your dog out if you must. Do three rights, then three lefts, accentuating the left signal. Soon your dog will catch on and you can mix it up: two rights, two lefts, two rights, one left, one right, and so on. Vary the pattern each time, and keep these mind puzzler sessions short. You'll also notice that your dog becomes clued in to your body language, and you can exaggerate the hand signal less and less.

Sarah Says

Another cool takeoff on Paw is Introduce Yourself (or Say Hello). Teach your dog the basic Paw, then just cue the same action on another command.

High Five

Okay hot shot, gimme five! This one is easy to teach and dogs love it.

Hold your hand, palm out, at the same height you normally ask for paw. If the command to "High Five" gets a puzzled look, then say "Paw" to request the action, and "High Five" as the dog's paw makes contact with your hand. Drop the Paw command when your dog makes the connection. Slowly lift your hand higher to accentuate the High Five.

Give me five, and keep it high!

Go for Ten

An extension of the High Five, Go for Ten involves two hands and two paws. When asking "Go for Ten," keep your hands at about the level of your dog's head. Any higher will encourage jumping.

Grrr

When asking for the High Five, stay within your dog's height capabilities. Don't encourage jumping. High Five is a three-paws-on-the-floor trick.

Remember that some dogs simply can't sit up on their hind legs. You'll know if your dog can't do this trick. So what? You love him anyway!

The High-Five Jig

High-Five Low-Five No-Five Shake! I first made up this
little jig to play with my niece and nephew, but who's to
say dogs won't love it just as much? The goal is to have a
good rhythmic movement, but start out slow and you can
work up to it.

> ➤ High Five: hold your hand high.

> ➤ Low Five: hold your hand low.

> ➤ No Five: purposely miss your dog's paw.

> ➤ Shake: extend your hand for a paw.

Snoopy Soccer

You'll need one or more players (plus your dog) and an
empty plastic soda bottle or a ball for each person and one
for the dog. Most dogs love to play with a ball or soda
bottle, wrestling and knocking it around with their feet.
They also love to use their mouth, which is fine if you just
want to mess around. If you're planning on teaching the
next four-legged soccer star, however, I suggest that you
get an indestructible ball made especially for dogs.

This is a goal-oriented game. Here's how to play:

> ➤ Get your dog interested in the bottle or ball by
> knocking it around gently.

> ➤ Interact in random patterns around a field.

> ➤ When your dog seems focused on this interaction,
> set up a six-foot-wide goal. Use trash cans, poles, or
> anything else you happen to have handy.

> ➤ Encourage your dog by saying "Goal" as you kick
> the bottle or ball toward the goal.

> ➤ Now for the clicker training we talked about in
> Chapter 2: Kick the ball or bottle to your dog and

say "Goal." Click and offer a treat for the slightest movement toward the goal.

➤ In the beginning, click and reward all movements toward the goal. Slowly space out the rewards, encouraging your dog further toward the goal before you reinforce him.

➤ Now it's time to go for the goal. Kick the bottle or ball toward your dog three feet in front of the goal and command "Goal!"

➤ The second your dog crosses the line with the bottle or ball, click and reward him!

➤ Now try passing the bottle or ball at farther distances from the goal. Pretty soon you can introduce him to the team!

Grrr

Be careful of your dog's face when kicking things around. If you're just playing soccer to fool around, use two balls and kick the one your dog's not playing with.

Hide and Seek

This is a great game and also reinforces that indispensable Come command. You need one to four players and a treat cup, and your dog needs to know his name and the Come command. Stay also comes in handy.

Start with this game inside, one-on-one. While your dog's occupied, go into an adjoining room with a treat cup. Call out his name and shake the cup. When you hear him running say "Come" clearly. Praise him, offer a treat, and let him return to whatever he was doing.

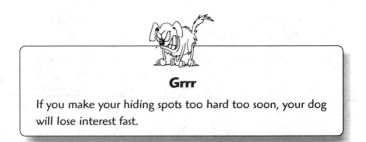

Grrr

If you make your hiding spots too hard too soon, your dog will lose interest fast.

After your dog aces this routine, increase the level of difficulty. Call him from two rooms away, but still be in sight, not hard to find. After a couple of days of hiding in plain sight around the house and calling from room to room, go into the adjoining room and hide behind a chair. Increase the difficulty of your hiding places and the distance from your dog as he catches on.

Now you can start playing hide and seek as a team sport. If your dog knows a solid "Stay," this is where it helps. Leave your dog in a Stay while you and another teammate or two hide (start off with easy-to-find hiding places). Decide who will call the dog first. After the dog is praised by the first person, have the second person give a holler.

After your dog catches on to this game, you can increase the difficulty of your hiding places and add another teammate. Eventually you two-legged geniuses can play a game to see who gets found first and who gets found last.

Catch Me

I've always hated games that involve people chasing dogs, especially when that game involved a coveted laundry item. Games that encourage your dog to focus on and follow you, however, are a real prize when it comes to training and having fun. These games also reinforce the extinction of bad habits, such as nipping and jumping. Here's how to play:

You need one or two players and a dog toy. Your dog needs to know Sit, Wait, Down, Stay, Okay, and No Sir/Ma'am.

➤ Turn and face your dog from about three to six feet away.

➤ Say "Catch Me," then turn and run.

➤ After a few feet, pop back to face your dog and command "Sit."

➤ Say "Okay" and "Catch Me," and run again.

➤ Pop back, turn, and give another stationary command such as "Wait."

➤ Follow each command with "Okay, Catch Me."

➤ Vary your commands and keep the game short, just one or two minutes.

➤ When you use the word "Stay," back away from your dog slowly, then say "Okay, Catch Me" to continue.

➤ When you're through, tell your dog "Okay" and give him a favorite toy.

I know I'll catch some slack for writing about this game. People are always asking if high-energy games encourage mouthing and jumping. My response? If it escalates the dog's bad behavior uncontrollably, leave it out. If your dog enjoys the game and you can curb naughtiness with a sharp "No Sir," then go for it. Catch Me is a fun activity and sharpens your dog's responsiveness to stationary commands.

Chapter 7

Mood Swings

In This Chapter

➤ Teach your dog to display a variety of moods

➤ Different ways of teaching high-energy and low-energy dogs

➤ How to keep training sessions short, simple, and fun

Here's a fine display of canine emotion. When your dog can act out each mood with style, you're really on your way to pleasing audiences everywhere. From happy to sad to doggone tired, teaching your dog these tricks is no small accomplishment.

Happy (Wag Your Tail)

This one is sooo easy! Say anything you want in a positive, inviting tone, and watch your dog come alive. Whenever I listen to clients complain about their dog, I turn to the dog and say, "Well, aren't you the naughtiest, most terrible little monster! What a nuisance you've become." I say it, however, in such a sweet, loving voice that it causes every dog to squirm with delight. The owners can't help but fall in love with their adoring (though confused) doggie all over again.

Sarah Says

Please notice that although hand signals are described for some tricks, you must first teach your dog how to do the trick before you can expect him to respond to a silent signal.

Try the following phrases on for size:

➤ If you're happy and you know it, wag your tail!

➤ Are you happy?

➤ Who's my best girl/boy?

If you're in front of a crowd, you can ask really difficult questions and tell your dog that if he agrees, all he has to do is wag his tail. It goes like this: "I'm going to ask you a hard question and if you agree all you have to do is wag your tail. Ready? Would you like everyone to give you a hug?"

Remember, all you have to do to get your dog to wag his tail is speak in the right tone. Practice right now!

Romantic (Kisses)

This one is a real delight, unless you hate dog kisses. You can teach this trick quickly by association, simply saying

"Kisses" whenever you're getting a licking. To teach your dog to give someone else a kiss, such as the next-door neighbor or a member of your audience, use a stick of butter during the teaching phase. Ask a few people to help you out, and rub the backs of their hands with butter before you instruct your dog to give them a kiss. Have them extend their hand to your dog and say "Kisses" as you point to the buttered hand. Soon your dog will be seeking out hands to kiss, butter-coated or not!

Sarah Says

Some dogs get really addicted to this game. If you can't get your dog to stop licking you or others, you'll need to teach "That's Enough." Keep a short tab (a very short loop of leash) on your dog and say "That's Enough" in a pleasant but serious tone, as you pull his head back from your hand.

Loving (Give Me a Hug)

To teach your dog to hug you, kneel down on the floor or sit in a chair. Give the Sit command and check to make sure your dog is sitting square on the floor (not leaning to either side). Next, lift your dog's paws gently and place them on your shoulders as you say "Hug." Give your dog a thorough petting and/or a reward. Then it's "Okay" and help him down. Repeat only three times per session, and stop if your dog is too energetic or starts to nip.

People always ask me if teaching a dog to hug will encourage him to jump. The answer is yes and no. Yes, it encourages jumping if your dog's already started the habit. No, it won't if you have taught your dog the Four Paw Rule: A well-mannered dog keeps four on the floor unless he's invited up. If you teach a jumping trick on cue, you can turn it off just as easily. It's the best of both worlds— selective spoiling.

Grrr

Some dogs get too excited standing on two paws. If this is your pal, leave the leash on and give a slight leash correction as you say "Shhh!" Also, try practicing Hug when your dog has less energy.

A hug is just what you need at the end of a long, hard day.

Polite (Ask Nicely)

Now we're getting into some more-serious maneuvers. This one is a real charmer, though, a variation on the old sit up and beg. To teach your dog this trick, I'll need to divide your dogs into three categories: the Naturals, the Corner Crew, and the Bowser Bracers.

The Naturals

These are the dogs who are most inclined to do this trick. They might have even discovered it by themselves during one of their more successful ploys to get attention. If not, you should have no trouble getting them to cooperate.

➤ Instruct "Sit" and make sure the dog is sitting squarely.

➤ Take a treat and hold it one inch above his nose.

➤ As he stretches to sniff it, bring it back slowly between his ears as you say "Ask Nicely."

➤ The dog should rise up to follow the path of the treat. Initially click and reward a split-second attempt to sit up. Once he's catching on, hold out for more-balanced performances.

Hand Signals

Move your palm upward, facing the sky.

The Corner Crew

These eager beavers are often coordinated enough, but are a little too excited about the thought of a biscuit. To structure the learning phase of this trick, follow the steps given previously but start the dog out in a corner of the room.

Tuck his back end toward the wall and proceed with train-ing. The walls on either side will help limit and guide his movements.

Bowser Bracers

If your dog is less than coordinated, you might need to be a more-active participant in the learning phase.

➤ Sit your dog squarely, instruct "Stay," and position yourself directly behind his tail.

➤ Hold the treat above his nose and bring it upward and back toward his ear.

➤ As you give the command and your dog begins to rise, brace his back with your legs for support.

➤ After initially clicking and rewarding the slightest lift, hold out for more-balanced (though still sup-ported) routines.

➤ When your dog can balance well with your help, be-gin to support him only with your knees.

➤ When he has perfected the trick with knee support, start withdrawing your support incrementally, until you are just standing there cheering your pal on.

Fairly soon you can begin to step away. See how he shines!

Sad (Head Down)

For this one your dog will lie down and place his head or nose between his paws and look up at you with a sad and soulful expression. Of course I'm not suggesting you actu-ally make your dog sad! It's just a trick.

Although they look sad, dogs are actually happy when they're doing tricks for you.

There are two ways to accomplish this maneuver, depending on how active your dog is.

Gentle Hold and Stay

If your dog's a real mush pie, she'll let you manipulate her head gently into position. First get your dog into a Down, and then position her head on the floor between her paws and instruct "Stay." Click if you're using a clicker; reward and praise a three-second stay, slowly increasing the time.

Hand Signals

Clasp your hands together under your chin.

Once your dog can hold herself in this position for ten seconds, start to introduce a word or phrase such as "Are you depressed?" or "Are you sad?" and have your dog show you by lying down and putting her head between her paws. What a heart stopper!

Lure Lassies

If your dog has no interest in sitting still and truly resists having you manipulate her head, you'll need to be more creative in your approach.

➤ Get your dog into a Down and Stay.

➤ Hold her favorite treat in your thumb, index, and middle fingers so that she can smell it but not eat it.

➤ Lure her head down between her paws using the treat and instruct "Stay." You may have to settle for a nose to the ground at first.

➤ Hold your hand still for three seconds, click, release, and praise. Slowly increase the time until your dog can be still for at least 15 seconds.

➤ Introduce your catch phrase while you are practicing the trick.

➤ Slowly wean your dog away from your presence on the floor, reward in hand, though you must always reward her for a job well done!

Tired (Go to Sleep)

When I was growing up, this trick was known as Play Dead. To me the whole dead thing seemed a little depressing; I prefer Go to Sleep—so much more peaceful.

Teaching this trick is not too hard if your dog has mastered the Down and Stay commands.

➤ Instruct "Down." Kneel and rub your dog's belly until she's calm.

➤ Gently roll your dog onto her side and command "Stay." If she lifts her head, lovingly rest it back on the floor and command "Stay."

➤ When your dog cooperates, start introducing your trick command, "Go to Sleep."

Hand Signals

Point with your index finger, as if to shoot.

Zany (Chase Your Tail)

A dog chasing his tail is a funny thing to watch, and no one can argue that he's truly mastered the art of having fun with himself. Whether your dog's a natural for this routine or not, it's not a hard one to teach.

Take a biscuit, hold it level with your dog's nose and command "Chase Your Tail" as you slowly rotate the treat around his body. I said slowly! Start slow; that's an order!

Hand Signals

Hold your index finger up and swirl it in a circle.

Reward half spins initially, then full spins, then two, three, four, and so on. Accentuate your hand signal, and soon you'll be sending your dog silent cues, no words needed!

Sarah Says

This trick is great if you want your dog to wipe his feet. Just command "Chase Your Tail" while he's standing on a doormat!

Sneezy

There are several reasons why you might want to teach your dog to sneeze on cue. First of all, what better way to bond than with a healthy sneeze-off between you two? And the next time you have guests over, you can ask your dog, "Who's your favorite dwarf?"

➤ Go to your dog and tell her "Sit."

➤ Blow into her nose gently from a distance of about two or three feet.

➤ This should encourage her to sneeze. When she does, pinch your nose with two fingers and say "Ahh-Choo!"

➤ If you're a theatrical sort, you'll be able to get your dog to sneeze with you for the fun of it. A sneeze-off!

➤ Soon try to get her to sneeze, hand signal only!

Hand Signals

Bow your head and gently pinch your nose with your thumb and index finger.

Embarrassed (Hide Your Face)

I've saved my toughest mood for last. But oh, how endearing to see your dog hide her face behind her paw. You'll teach this trick so that your dog will respond to a hand signal only, and you can lead up to it with questions like "How do you feel when I catch you on the counter?" or "Would you like some beans with your dinner?" or "I heard you met a fancy Poodle the other day . . . ."

Getting your dog to do this one is a real art form. First you must get her in a calm, cooperative mood. If she's got too much energy, she'll quickly get frustrated and quit. Next you must practice your Paw command. Now you're ready to begin.

➤ Take your dog into a quiet area and tell her "Sit."

➤ Practice a few Paw commands.

➤ Hold a treat down low and on the opposite side of the paw your dog has been giving you. In other words, if your dog has been giving you her right paw, hold the treat to her left side.

➤ You may need to gently hold the skin below her neck to brace her head into position as her paw comes up.

➤ When her paw and nose meet, mark the moment with a click or a "Yes!" and reward and praise.

➤ Stop after she makes three contacts, rewarding the session generously with a favorite game.

➤ Do not practice more than four sessions a day.

Hand Signals

Cuff the side of your nose.

If your dog is clueless with this procedure, you'll need to get more ingenious with your training techniques. This is what I call the induced training method.

➤ Take your dog into a quiet area and instruct "Sit."

➤ Have on hand your treat rewards and your clicker.

➤ Stick a little loop of cellophane tape lightly to the side of your dog's nose.

➤ When he lifts his paw to knock it off, click, reward, and praise.

➤ When your dog catches onto the game, start to introduce a command such as Hide Your Face and blatantly scratch the side of your nose as a hand signal.

➤ Initially reward your dog regardless of the position he gets into as she tries to remove the tape from her nose. Gradually shape the behavior to what you're looking for.

Grrr

Use only cellophane tape, and stick it on very lightly. You don't want to hurt your dog by pulling out her hair along with the tape.

Now you're ready for show time. Practice this one in more and more distracting areas before inviting an audience to witness your brilliant pal at work.

Mix and Match

Be creative when teaching your dog these tricks. If you can tie in a unique hand signal, your dog will not only learn to watch you better but will also perform happily with no words needed.

Now you can really start having some fun! For example, after you ask your dog which is his favorite dwarf and he sneezes, follow up by asking about his least-favorite dwarf and give the Go to Sleep command.

Chapter 8

Everyday Miracles

In This Chapter

➤ Teaching your dog to potty in one designated place

➤ Settling down for a rest

➤ Picking up, doggy style

➤ Closing cupboards, Say Your Prayers, and more

This chapter is about manners. While every dog should have the basic good manners to sit, stay, not jump, and not pull, you can invite a really mannerly dog to dinner, and she will know exactly which fork to use. In fact, these tricks are so mannerly and endearing that you can take your dog to dinner with the Queen.

Potty in One Place

No small miracle! And your dog must be fully housebroken before you attempt this little trick. This is what I want you to do:

➤ Select a sacred Bathroom Area in your yard.

➤ Take your dog to the specific spot, first thing in the morning. When she goes, praise and treat (the clicker is optional).

➤ Find some thick white clothesline and lay it out in a six-foot circle around your dog's elimination.

➤ Next time you take your dog out to potty, go to this area and ignore your dog.

➤ If your dog goes potty in the circle, click and treat. If not, praise calmly but no treat.

If your dog decides to play with the rope, soak it overnight in Bitter Apple Spray (found in local pet supply stores), a nontoxic substance with a taste dogs find unpleasant. Have faith! Soon your dog will be as potty trained as a six-year-old.

Grrr

Do not leave more than one elimination in the circle, and as soon as your dog learns this trick, pick up *everything* promptly. No dog will go where she's gone twenty times before. Would you?

City Canines

So you don't have a three-acre spread in the country. Don't feel bad. The circle trick can work for you too;

you'll just need to shrink your circumference and curb it: That's the law! Your dog may even need to adjust to a shape other than a circle, but the plan is similar: Reward deposits made inside the rope, lightly praise those done outside.

Paper Plans

Got an indoor dog? The circle trick may not be necessary, as your dog will usually go wherever the paper is placed. If you're a seasoned traveler, however, a portable rope outlining the paper can help ease the travel transition for your dog.

Settle in One Spot

This is one of those lessons you appreciate for the rest of your life. Pick an area for your dog in each room. I advise a spot that is to the side or in a quiet corner; in my other books I refer to it as a station. Adorn your dog's station with a toy and bedding, if that's what she likes.

Each time you are in the room and you'd like your dog to quiet down, instruct her "Settle Down" as you point to her area. If she ignores you, lead her there and say "Settle" as you position her in a comfortable Down and instruct "Stay." If your dog challenges her Stay command, secure a leash to an immovable object near the station, leaving just enough slack for your dog to lie down comfortably.

Sarah Says

Betcha haven't thought of this one! If you've got small kids, or if your dog's still a pup, attach your dog's toy to a piece of rope and tie it to something immovable near the station spot. That way it won't disappear.

Soon you'll be able to point and your dog will go happily, content to chew her favorite toy and stay out from underfoot. If you'd like to create a permanent doggy spot in the TV room or the bedroom, consider placing it near your couch or bed. Dogs love being close!

Tell Me You're Hungry

Growing up, I had a Collie named Meghan who was my pride and joy. I remember saving every dollar I had until there was enough to buy her. One of her most endearing qualities was to bring me gifts. If I was happy, she'd always bring over a ball to play. If I had a bad day, I could always count on Meghan greeting me at the bus with a leaf or twig or some other earthly treasure. And heaven forbid I was two minutes late to feed her, she would always drop her food dish in my lap.

How do you teach your dog this charming little trick? You need to start out with a dog that is comfortable putting things in her mouth. If your dog won't pick up anything short of a biscuit, then she might not be the best candidate.

Are you still with me? Let's proceed:

➤ Take your dog aside with treats and her food dish. If you're using a stainless steel bowl (which I recommend), tie a cotton cloth around the rim.

➤ Ask your dog, "Are you hungry?" and wave the bowl in front of her face. When she clamps on, praise, click, and treat.

➤ Practice until your dog makes the connection that grasping the bowl is the name of the game.

➤ Now hold the bowl closer to the floor. Lift the bowl an inch from the floor and swish it back and forth as you ask, "Are you hungry?" When the dog takes the bowl, click if you're using a clicker, and reward.

➤ Drumroll please! Place the bowl on the floor, stand up straight and ask, "Are you hungry?" Praise any interest your dog shows in the bowl. Reward any contact.

➤ As the light flashes in your dog's head, begin to ask the dog to Come, and gently take the bowl from her mouth. Eventually, reward only deliveries.

Grrr

Do not play this game at feeding time or with your dog's bowl full of food. You do *not* want to teach her to snatch her food bowl from your hand.

Pick Up Your Toys

Always shopping for your dog? Well don't feel bad; I'm a bit of a toy freak myself. My favorites are the animal toys that sound like the animals themselves: a cow that moos, a frog that ribbets, a pig that oinks. Guess I'm easily amused.

If your house has begun to look like a mine field, you might want to teach your dog Tidy Up!

➤ First you'll need a toy box and a designated area set aside for it. It's a big decision; you can't change its location for a while.

➤ Bring your dog to his box with a favorite toy.

➤ Give him the toy.

➤ Snap your fingers over the box. When your dog leans his head over the box, tell him "Drop, Tidy

Up," click, and offer a treat (which should encourage your dog to drop the toy).

➤ Repeat this four times.

➤ Stop and remove the box.

➤ Repeat these sessions once or twice a day.

➤ As your dog catches on, try giving him the toy farther and farther from his box (which should always be in the same area).

➤ After he catches onto this step, go near the box again, but this time leave the toy on the floor and encourage your dog to pick it up.

➤ Now try for two toys. Start by rewarding only a two-toy drop, then a three-toy drop, then a four.

Hand Signals

Sweep the room with an outstretched finger.

Now you're ready to start hiring out your very own four-footed maid service!

Open and Shut

Teaching your dog to open and shut the cupboards is one clever act, but it's two separate skills, and you have to teach them one by one.

Shutting Doors

This trick requires the Touch command (remember it from Chapter 2?). Review it if necessary. It's best to use a clicker or some other device.

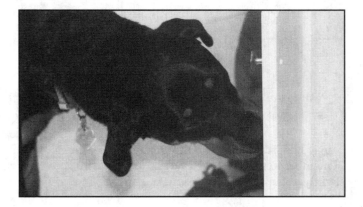

Teaching your dog to shut the cupboard door is just a variation of that old trick, Touch.

➤ Hold out a greeting card or an index card to your dog and say "Touch." Click, treat, and praise.

➤ Move around the room, holding the card in various locations, giving the Touch command. Don't move to the next step until your dog has got this one down pat.

➤ Drumroll please. Tape the card to a cupboard door and open the door slightly. Tape the card at your dog's chin level. Nothing too high; nothing too low.

➤ Command "Touch," and reward the slightest effort, even if your dog doesn't shut the cupboard completely.

➤ As your dog catches on, open the door and command "Shut It" as you point to the cupboard door. Reward only those touches that snap the cupboard tightly closed.

Hand Signals

Point to the intended door or cupboard.

Now you're ready to expand to other doors in the house. Remember to start each new adventure with the door only slightly open, and progress slowly.

Opening Doors

When teaching this command I usually divide dogs into two categories: paw or mouth expressive. Either way, you'll need to make a rope handle and attach it to the door at either paw or mouth height.

Mouth Expressive: First, wiggle the rope and pique your dog's interest away from the door. When your dog starts mouthing the rope, attach it to the door handle and reward your dog for pulling it on location.

Paw Expressive: Attach the rope to the door handle, pretend to paw at it, and reward your dog for copying you. Once you've piqued your dog's interest, follow this series of steps:

➤ At first, reward each contact with the rope.

➤ Then reward only those contacts that open the door slightly.

➤ Finally, reward only those contacts that fully open the door.

Now you've got a dog who can not only open the cupboard to take what she wants but who can cover her tracks by closing it!

Get Your Leash

It's a fact of nature that dogs love to go for walks. To teach them this little trick might be inviting some late-night leash deliveries, but you decide. I think bringing a leash is pretty ingenious, and it's a simple trick to master. Here we go!

➤ When your dog is not wearing her leash, encourage her to take it in her mouth.

➤ When she'll do it readily, say "Get Your Leash!" and click and treat.

➤ Fold the leash neatly and secure it with a rubber band or string. Place it on the couch and encourage your dog to get it by saying "Get Your Leash!" and pointing to it.

➤ If your dog grabs it, click and treat (even for only a partial return).

➤ Repeat the preceding step, but only reward when your dog brings the leash to you.

➤ Remove the string and let your dog drag the leash to you. Its weight and pull may seem awkward at first, but praise your dog as you encourage her to come to you.

Grrr

It's fine for your dog to bring her leash to ask for a walk, but *never* let her mouth it when she's wearing it. Dogs that take their leash in their mouth during a walk are trying to wrest control from you. *You* should be walking your dog; don't allow her to walk herself.

➤ Go to the area where you keep the leash and place it in an obvious spot. Stand just a few feet away and encourage your dog's delivery.

➤ Extend your distance from the leash as you repeat the request, and reward good deliveries.

Leap Dog

It's no secret, dogs love to jump: on guests, counters, family members, each other—it's all one big game. But for those of you who are less than delighted at your dog's enthusiasm for standing on two paws, read closely. The best way to teach your dog when not to jump is to teach her when she can jump. Redirect that enthusiasm, and put it on cue. Here's how.

Over

Structured jumping must start somewhere, so here we go. Get a broom or a straight pole. In a carpeted area, balance the pole on two objects of equal height. Make sure it's secure enough so that it can't be easily knocked over.

How high should the pole be? To start, measure the height between your dog's paw and his shoulder. Divide this in half, then subtract an inch. That's how high your training jump should be. (Later, when your dog learns this trick, you can make it higher.)

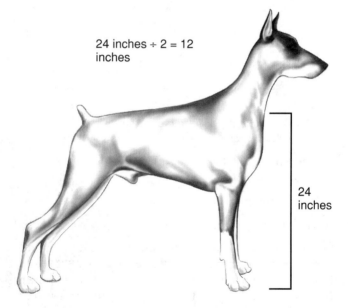

24 inches ÷ 2 = 12 inches

24 inches

The training jump for this dog should be 11 inches.

Now you're ready to begin. Place your dog on a short leash for control.

➤ Let your dog sniff the jump. Discourage any test chewing with a light "Ep, ep."

➤ Bring your dog back and say "Over" before you move toward the jump.

➤ Jog up lightly and jump just ahead of your dog.

➤ If your dog refuses, stay calm. Walk over the jump several times while your dog watches, then try to walk over it together. It may take a few goes, but your dog will soon overcome her fears.

➤ Now, pick up the pace. Move at your dog's natural gait, not too fast and not too slow.

➤ Once your dog takes the jump with pride, stop just before the jump and let your dog do it alone. Reward with a jackpot of treats and praise.

➤ Stop your approach farther and farther back from the jump. Say "Over" before you send your dog, pointing to the intended obstacle.

Hand Signals

Sweep your arm toward the jump.

When you're still teaching this trick, walk over the jump right behind your dog and praise her before she has a chance to turn back and retrace her path to you.

Once your dog learns how to jump properly, you can raise the jump to a height appropriate to your dog. Set up an obstacle course, directing your dog to each jump with a sweep of your arm. Set up jumps in your driveway, yard, or a nearby park. Practice your Over command when you come across a natural obstacle, such as a railing or a fallen branch.

Grrr

Never raise a jump higher than one-and-a-half times your dog's height, and remember many dogs will be comfortable jumping only at lower heights.

Over the Kids

Kids also make good natural obstacles (as any parent will tell you). And while kids don't exactly get into the Sit, Stay, and Come exercises, they do like to join in fun tricks with their dog.

For this trick, have the kids and the dog practice Over with the broom so the dog gets used to performing around the children. The next step will depend on how many kids you've got.

One Kid: Ask your child to lie down under or alongside the jump. Take your dog and let her sniff the new setup. Say "Ep, ep" if she gets excited and lead her back five strides. Say "Over," run toward the jump, and leap together. Send your dog alone once she cooperates.

Slowly encourage your child to raise her back toward the ceiling until you find the right height for your dog. When your child has friends visiting you can add another child.

More Than One Kid: Always start the kid jump with one child, as described previously. If you want to add children, first let the dog jump over them one at a time, just to get used to each child. Then begin to line the kids out flat, on either side of the broom jump. One at a time they should raise their backs to a height that's comfortable for your dog. Be realistic though: Don't add so many kids that your dog is forced to step over them like rocks across a stream.

Through

Jumping through something is a natural progression from Over and really adds zing to any trick routine (make sure your dog really is comfortable with Over before you try Through). Your dog can jump through a hoop, into your arms, or through a car window.

The Hoop

Let's start with the hoop. Go out to your local variety store and dig a hula hoop out of the corner. Though its place on the shelf has been taken by electronic pastimes, you can still find a hula hoop if you look hard enough.

Set up your original jumping pole across a threshold or between two pieces of furniture. Put your dog on a short lead, and let her sniff the hoop as you position it on the floor in the center of the jump. Ask someone to hold the hoop or prop it up securely. Instruct your dog "Over" as you run toward the obstacle, letting go of the hand lead as you get close.

After your dog cooperates, start adding the command Through as you start for the jump, like this: "Over, Through."

Next, hold or prop the hoop higher so it is even with the height of the pole. Now your dog might hesitate because the hoop looks, well, like a hoop, not like a level jump. If this is the case, approach it slowly and let your dog walk through it a couple of times, using food to encourage her.

Now you're ready to try the hoop alone. Using another threshold or restricted area, prop or hold the hoop securely on the floor. Instructing "Through," trot up to the jump and let your dog go through alone. Praise her joyously and encourage her to go back through by running backward yourself. Clap, sing, praise, treat—let your dog know what a star she is!

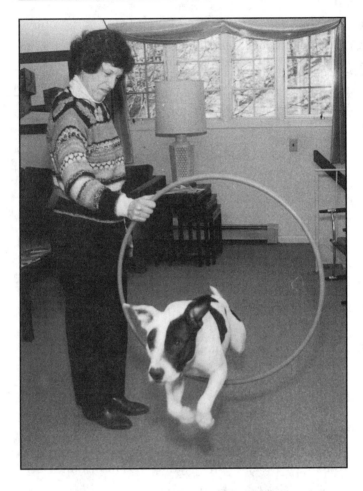

This is a lot more fun than trying to wiggle this hoop around your waist.

Progressively raise the hoop to a height appropriate for your dog. Once she's comfortable with this routine in a restricted area, start working her in more-open areas. Keep your praise and energy high; this display is a real crowd pleaser.

Sarah Says

If your dog refuses the hoop, let her watch as you climb in and out cheerfully. Standing on one side, toss a cherished treat through to the other side and lead your dog through calmly.

Your Arms

If you have a small-to-medium dog, this trick is a heart warmer. If you're truly daring you can try it with a large dog, but let me warn you: Watch out for your nose. One of my brightest students, a chipper Chocolate Lab, had mastered every trick I knew, so I decided to give this trick a try. Of course, once he figured out what I wanted he was eager to give it his all. Unfortunately, one day my nose got in the way and there was blood everywhere. Poor boy—he thought he'd killed me.

➤ Approach this trick as with the hoop, placing your arms in a hoop shape with one elbow on the floor.

➤ It's easier to have an extra person around to lure your dog through your arms with a treat as you say "Through." But if you want to try it solo, place your dog in a Stay on one side of a doorway, show him a treat, toss it to the other side of the doorway, and release with "Okay, Through" as you position your arms.

➤ Your praise must be ecstatic and uplifting. What a great dog you have!

➤ Progressively hold your arms higher and slowly work out of the restrictions of the doorway.

Into

Dogs, being dogs, love to jump into things. In fact, sometimes the real trick is getting them to jump out. (More on that later.) The hardest decision for me was where to start this section.

Your Lap

Dogs love laps. Getting them to jump there, however, is a stunt that is somewhat restricted by size. Avoid this trick if your dog weighs more than you or weighs under five pounds. Small dogs have big hearts but short legs; don't push them.

➤ Put your dog in a Stay across the room. Show your dog her favorite toy or treat.

➤ Sit in a low chair. Patting your lap say "Name" and "Come," then "Up."

➤ The first time you try this, the dog may run over and stop short or put two paws up. Praise and offer a treat anyway, and lead her back to the starting point. Reward any attempts to join you the first three tries.

➤ Eventually, reward only for landing in your lap.

Hand Signals

Pat your lap.

Is your dog earthbound in disbelief? The next time she approaches, gently grasp her collar under her chin and ease her up. Reward that. Soon she'll be leaping at your invitation.

A Chair

Are those sad hound dog eyes melting your heart while you're trying to eat? Among my many options for handling dogs and dining, let me add this one to the list: a formal invitation.

> ➤ Attach a piece of carpet or toweling to a dining chair (for better footing).

> ➤ Encourage your dog onto the chair by saying something funny, such as "Dinner Time," as you pat the chair and help your dog onto the seat.

> ➤ Because dogs like to be up, you should have no problem convincing your dog that this is the place to be, but now you'll need her to sit still while you push in her chair. Try using the Stay command, moving the chair in little by little.

Of course, now that your dog is sitting at the dinner table, it's your job to figure out what to do with her.

Up into Your Arms

To get your dog to do this trick, start out kneeling in front of her, encouraging her up to your face with your arms extended. She'll probably use your body like a ladder; be prepared. Next, leave your dog in a Stay across the room while you continue to kneel in a low position. Call her with "Come, Up!" Praise like mad when she ends up in your arms.

Hand Signals

Bend your knees and pat your thighs.

After your dog catches on to the run and jump, begin to rise slowly. Soon your dog will jump into your arms for the sheer delight of a kiss.

Chapter 10

Noisy Tricks

In This Chapter

➤ Teaching your dog to bark on cue

➤ Teaching your dog not to bark on cue

➤ Sounding the alarm, singing, counting, and more

➤ Redeeming the problem barker

Does your dog love to make noise? Does he bark when he's happy, excited, when he doesn't get his way? Is your biggest question not how to train him to be vocal, but how to shut it off? Actually, it's easier than you think. You start by training him to do something he already likes to do: bark! Then you can turn him on and off.

Once you have a greater appreciation for your dog's natural vocal talents, you'll need to do a little coaching. Are you ready Maestro?

Ready on Four

To teach your dog to bark on command, you'll need to use eye contact, hand signals, and voice commands.

Eye Contact: Look at your dog alertly when you want him to bark. Break your stare when you want him to quiet down.

Voice Commands: You'll need two—Speak and Shhh. Enunciate clearly when you give your commands.

Hand Signals

You need a snappy hand signal for Speak; try snapping your fingers near your mouth. For Shhh, put your index finger to your lips as if you were shushing a baby.

Lesson One. Get something your dog lives for—a ball or treat for example. Secure him to a post or tree and hold his prized object just out of reach while you encourage "Speak" and look at him intensely. When he does bark, reward him cheerfully. Begin to add the hand signal to your voice and eye cues. Repeat this procedure until your dog reacts quickly to the Speak command.

Lesson Two. Encourage your dog to speak throughout the day for positive things, such as a meal or a walk. If he speaks out of turn, just ignore him.

Lesson Three. Now it's time to turn your dog's focus to Shhh. Go back to Lesson One, securing him and standing in front of him with something tasty or fun. Say "Speak!" After a few barks say "Shhh," stamp your foot and avert your eyes. Click, if you're using a clicker, reward, and praise. Repeat this process until your dog responds to both Speak and Shhh.

Lesson Four. Practice your commands throughout the day, varying which ones you reinforce. Sometimes reward the Speak, sometimes the Shhh. Have your dog Speak and Shhh two or three times before rewarding him. He'll be so proud of his new trick, and so will you!

Sarahs Says

After your dog learns Speak, Bark to Go Out is a really simple variation. Start first thing in the morning when your dog really has to go. Go to the door, tell her "Speak," and don't open the door until she does. What's the secret password?

Alarm Dog

Believe it or not, some dogs don't bark when the doorbell rings. But even if yours does, teaching her to bark on cue will also help her stop barking (there's more on problem barkers at the end of this chapter). To help your dog learn to bark when the doorbell rings, ring it yourself.

➤ Put your dog on a Sit-Stay and stand at the open door.

➤ Ring the bell and command "Speak"; click and reward the inevitable bark.

➤ Ring the bell again, instruct "Speak," but wait until your dog responds to "Shhh" before you reward her.

➤ Now ask a neighbor to come by and ring the bell or knock when your dog is not expecting company. Re-inforce Speak or Shhh—whichever happens to be your dog's weak suit.

➤ Repeat the process in your car. While the car is parked in the driveway, have someone approach, telling your dog to bark on cue. As your dog learns this one, you can gradually work up to parking lots and even gas stations.

Singing the Blues

Some dogs just sing the blues naturally. The arctic breeds, shepherds, and hound dogs are notorious for letting out a howl when they hear music or get excited. Others you can teach to sing.

Monkey see, monkey do applies here. Play some soulful music and let out a good howl yourself. Toss your head back and hit the high notes! Whether your dog joins in this session or the next, let yourself go and end by playing your dog's favorite game. Soon his tail will beat the floor whenever you pass by the stereo.

When your dog joins in, congratulate him and keep on howling. To signal a howl, lean your head back, face to the moon, and purse those lips. Now you can think of clever questions to ask your dog. What does a werewolf do when he sees a full moon? What do you say when you see your girlfriend/boyfriend? Clever dog!

Counting and Other Complex Math Problems

This is where your bark-training efforts really pay off. People will be thrilled to see your dog doing better in math than they did in high school.

Singing the blues is a natural for the arctic breeds.

Before you start asking your dog to count anything, you must polish his Speak and Shhh skills, so he can do them with hand signals alone (if you give the voice commands, some doubters may believe it's not really your dog who's counting). Once you've got the commands down pat, you can begin asking your dog some basic questions. Just give the Speak hand signal, count the barks, and then signal "Shhh." Try these to start:

➤ How much is two plus two?

➤ How old are you?

➤ How many eggs in a half dozen?

Work on your silent communication, so that no one can tell you're helping out. Once your dog can answer the basics, you can proceed to more difficult math problems:

➤ How many stars in the Big Dipper? (The answer is seven.)

➤ What's the square root of 64? (You should know this one!)

➤ If two sides of a right triangle are each two inches long, how many inches long is the third side? (Three, of course—let your dog round off the decimal.)

The Bothersome Barker

A barking dog is a real headache. How you handle your situation will depend on what is prompting your dog to bark in the first place. But whatever you do, don't yell. Yelling is barking in Doglish, and instead of calming your dog it will rile him up. To solve your problem, stay cool. Let's break up the barkers into categories.

Grrr

Never hold your dog back while you open the door. It's like holding a frantic child; it will only make him more wild. Also, approach the door calmly. Running to the door and screaming at your dog will create a frenzy.

At the Door

Almost everyone appreciates a dog alarm at the door; a few woofs announce new arrivals. It gets annoying, however, when the alarm can't be shut off. After all, enough is enough. The ideal situation is to have an alarm bark with an off switch. Here's how:

➤ Place a penny can and a clicker or treat cup at the door.

➤ Position someone outside the door and ask the person to ring the bell 10 times every 20 seconds.

➤ When your dog starts barking, say "Speak" and approach the door calmly. Praise him and then say "Shhh."

➤ If necessary, support your command with a shake of the penny can. (You may even need to let your dog drag a hand leash to snap a little sense into him!) Click, treat, and praise your dog when he quiets down.

➤ Repeat and repeat until your dog gets the hang of it. Now try it with a real guest.

Sarah Says

To make a penny can, fill an empty soda can with ten pennies and tape the top. The shaking sound startles dogs.

Motion Detector

Got one of those dogs who barks at everything she sees and hears? This type of barking can be really rewarding for your dog because whenever she barks at something, whether from the window or the yard, it goes away.

How do you remedy your motion detector?

➤ Avoid leaving your dog alone outdoors for long stretches of time. Confinement often breeds boredom and territorial behavior. Put those two together and you're likely to end up with a barkaholic.

➤ Don't yell; screaming is barking in Doglish. Your dog will feel supported, not discouraged.

➤ Anytime you see (or hear) your dog start to perk up, say "Shhh" and use your clicker or treat cup to encourage her to come. If your dog ignores you, leave a hand lead on her collar and use it for reinforcement. If necessary, use a penny can to help break your dog's focus.

➤ If your fellow is a night watchman, you'll need to station him in your room. Give him a bed and a bone, and secure his lead to something stationary. Bedtime!

➤ Last but not least, give your dog an outlet for barking by teaching the noisy tricks outlined in this chapter.

Sarah Says

Dogs who bark at everything perceive themselves as your leader. One of the leader's duties is to guard his territory and pack from intruders. All the other training and interaction you're doing will help your dog focus on and respect you as the leader of the pack. That's important; without that, you'll be hard pressed to make any impression.

Attention Hound

Imagine this: You're sitting reading the Sunday paper when suddenly your dog comes out of nowhere and starts barking for a pat. Cute, huh? Not really. So what should you do? Giving in would make you look like a servant. Yelling would be counterproductive. Got any ideas? Here are two:

➤ Occasionally, turn to your dog and instruct "Speak!" Let him bark a couple of times, then say "Shhh" and ignore him. Walk away if you need to, but don't give in and pay attention.

➤ When your dog is barking for attention, that's the time to ignore her. Otherwise, you're teaching her that barking is a very effective tool. I know, it may give you a headache, but let me suggest wax ear-plugs. They work wonders.

Protest Barking

Some dogs don't like to be left alone. To tell you the truth, neither do I. If you return and soothe a protest barker, you'll end up with a really spoiled dog on your hands—one who has trained you.

On the other hand, if you ignore the protest barking, your neighbors, or even your spouse may protest. Is there a happy medium? Not really, but I'll give you some suggestions.

➤ Ignore it if you can. Never yell.

➤ Avoid grand departures and arrivals; they're too stimulating.

➤ Dogs like to be with you. When you're home, let them.

➤ Place peanut butter in a hollow rubber bone and give it to your dog as you leave. It's a tasty way to keep him busy!

➤ Return to your dog only after he's calmed down. If you must interfere with his barking tantrum, go quietly without eye contact or comments, place him on the teaching lead tied around your waist and ignore him for half an hour while you lead him around.

The K–9 Express

Having a retriever in your home has many perks: the fun of fetch, a helper to carry in the groceries, slippers delivered to your chilly feet. There are few things as astounding as seeing this kind of dog in action. On the other hand, there is nothing funnier than the retriever turned inside out: the comic fellow who runs away from you or brings things back just out of reach.

In reality, there is not too much distance between the cooperative retriever and the ham. Both are thinking of their owner when they have something in their mouth. The Good Retriever has been taught to share. Mister

Comedian has been taught that treasures are best kept to oneself. Of course, not everybody loves a comedian.

Labrador Retrievers will fetch through rain, snow, sleet, hail, and water.

It's a Gene Thing

The instinct to retrieve is all in the genes. For example, my Labrador Retriever Calvin would retrieve until I was begging him for a break. My Husky Kyia, on the other hand, would show me the funniest expression when I tossed a ball for her. If she could talk, I'm sure she'd say to me, "And you expect me to bring that back to you? Not!"

If you're sitting across from a dog who won't fetch your ball, don't feel bad. Some dogs were called for other wonders. In truth, I could have trained Kyia to retrieve, but I would have had to use unnatural or harsh methods. In her lifetime I never forced Kyia to do anything that didn't agree with her natural instincts.

There also are exceptions to the gene rule. In fact, I know a purebred Husky who would put most retrievers to shame.

Of course, there are other dogs with the genes and the potential to make good retrievers who won't give the ball back to you. Many have elevated the game of Keep Away to an art. If this is your pal, there's hope. To teach a full retrieve—go out, bring it back, and give it up—each of the steps must be taught individually before they're brought together.

Sarah Says

If you are planning to compete in formal Obedience trials with your nonretrieving dog and you must teach the fetch, try the methods outlined in the next section. If they are ineffective, there are many good show ring Obedience books that will describe other methods you can try.

Bring It Back

Anything a dog puts in his mouth is special, at least to him. So the first step in teaching the retrieve is to get your dog psyched to show you his "treasure." All your dog must do to learn this step is come back with his prize. The focus here is on the Bring, not the Give.

➤ Line up several toys, a clicker if you're using one, and treats.

➤ Gently toss a toy a few feet away from you. Each time your dog brings you a toy, shower him with praise but don't take the toy away.

➤ As your dog catches on and trots back to you happily, say "Bring."

➤ When your dog arrives, toy in mouth, praise and pet him heartily (click and treat if you like), leaving the object in his mouth. Return to your stack and toss a different toy.

➤ If your dog ignores you when he gets the toy, try running away from him after he's picked it up. If he still won't bring it back, pretend to eat some of his treat. When he brings it over, shower him with love but don't reach for the toy just yet.

➤ After your dog is bringing his toy in on the Bring command, you're ready for step two: Give.

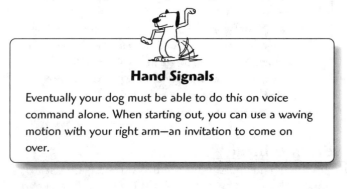

Hand Signals

Eventually your dog must be able to do this on voice command alone. When starting out, you can use a waving motion with your right arm—an invitation to come on over.

Give It Up

Parting is such sweet sorrow. Relinquishing an object is the trickiest part of the retrieve, especially if you've chased your dog for things in the past. Be patient. Follow the steps, and be smart enough not to lose your temper if your dog is trying to outsmart you. A graceful retreat is not a failure.

Give with Treats

No more chasing. That's final. Instead, offer something better.

➤ Pull up a chair and line up your clicker, some treats, and your dog's favorite toy.

➤ Call your dog over, show him the toy, and praise him when he takes it.

➤ Next, with a treat and clicker in hand, say "Give." The treat should induce him to drop the toy. Click and reward the second he releases it.

➤ Now go to a hallway or an enclosed space. Toss the toy.

➤ Praise your dog the moment he picks it up; go to him and say "Give" as you click and reward the release.

Hand Signals

Hold your open palm in front of your dog's mouth.

You may notice that your dog releases the ball as you approach or tosses it on the ground near you. Although this is acceptable when starting out, you'll eventually need to be more selective with your rewards. Deliveries are to be made mouth to hand. Here's how to shape this behavior:

➤ Go back to your chair.

➤ Give your dog the toy and say "Give" as you extend your hand under your dog's mouth.

➤ If your dog tosses it on the ground, ignore the result and begin again.

➤ Click and reward the moment the toy drops into your hand.

Give Without Treats

Some dogs are so obsessed that they can't think of anything else. If this sounds like your fellow and you're having a rough time getting his attention with treats around, you'll need to teach him without treats.

It's not so hard. Follow the steps outlined previously, simply inserting an extra helping of praise where it says to click and reward with a treat.

Grrr

Avoid overdoing it. Don't toss objects all day, saying "Bring, Bring, Bring," or you'll find your dog avoiding you, saying, "Not, Not, Not!"

Bring and Give

Once your dog learns that when you say "Bring," you want the object you pointed to and when you say "Give," it's a hand delivery you're looking for, you're ready to connect the two talents.

➤ Go to a hallway or enclosed space.

➤ Give the toy a short toss and instruct "Bring." When your dog grabs it, cheer him back to you.

➤ Extend your hand to retrieve the object, "Give," and reward your dog for a job well done! Repeat this twice, and then quit while you're ahead.

> If your dog gets so excited that he can't hold onto the toy, you might be rushing it. Go back to the earlier steps and progress slowly.

Sarah Says

Is your dog so mouthy that he's into carrying anything that moves, including your undergarments, remote control, or soap? Place treat cups throughout the house, and each time he steals, shake the cup and encourage "Bring." Now you'll have a resident delivery service instead of a one-dog wrecking crew.

Retrieving Dowels and Dumbbells

If you plan to enter your dog in an Obedience competition, you'll need to be a bit more formal with your choice of toys to play with; actually, serious competitors would be hesitant to call the equipment they use toys. To be specific, you'll need to practice with dowels and dumbbells.

A dowel is a piece of wood shaped like a stick, but it is more regular in shape and uniform in length. The dumbbell used in formal Obedience work looks like a small dumbbell you'd find at your gym, but it's made of wood.

Start your formal retrieving work with a dowel. Take your dog into a quiet room and line up your clicker, some treats, and your dowel. Again we'll break down the exercise into parts, but this time we'll go in reverse.

Take It

Present your dog with the dowel and say "Take It." If he takes it, praise him, click, and reward. (This step may take

some time and some enticing. Make that dowel look inter-
esting!) Soon your dog will take it readily. Now you're
ready for the second step.

Grrr

Don't hold the dowel above your dog's head; you don't
want to encourage jumping.

Hold

Now ask your dog to Hold the dowel as you put it in front
of his muzzley mug. At first he'll probably spit it out;
ignore that. Present the dowel again and hold it gently in
his mouth as you repeat "Hold." Click and reward.

Hand Signals

When you ask your dog to Hold, point your finger close to
his nose.

Slowly progress until your dog holds the dowel for thirty
seconds. Don't worry if the seasons change while you're
perfecting this exercise. I had a Collie who took almost six
months to fully grasp it.

Most dogs think the dowel is just another chew toy.
That's why I like to start with the dowel (so you can break
the habit) before you start working with the dumbbell.

When your dog starts to roll the dowel in his mouth and chew, use your gentle discouraging words, "Ep, ep." If that doesn't impress him, snap his leash gently, "Ep, ep," and don't click and reward. Don't get mad, however, or you'll discourage your dog from ever retrieving for you again.

Before progressing to the next step, introduce your dog to the dumbbell. It will feel funny at first (the ends are weighted), and your dog may roll it around in his mouth, but discourage this with a light "Ep, ep."

Send

Now you'll need to teach your dog to go out and retrieve the dumbbell for you. In previous games you conditioned him to think retrieving was cool, so this step shouldn't a big deal.

➤ Begin by holding the dumbbell level with the dog's face and about a foot away from him. Tell your dog "Take It," encouraging him to reach for the dumbbell.

➤ Work the two-inch rule, lowering the dumbbell toward the floor two inches at a time. Encourage your dog to Take It on command each time.

➤ When you get to the floor, keep your hand under the dumbbell and shake it lightly. Release it after your dog takes it quickly, and slowly return to a standing position.

➤ Next, put your dog in a Stay, place the dumbbell in front of you on the floor, then send him to Take It. The one-foot rule is the name of this game. Have the dog Stay, put the dumbbell down one foot away, then return to him, and command "Take It."

➤ Move the dumbbell out one foot at a time. Once you're three feet away, you'll find that you can progress more quickly.

Carry This, Carry That

Back when I had an office in town, it was a common spectacle to see my Labrador Calvin walking at my side carrying my lunch bag. Everybody joked that the bag was empty, but I'd bet my business and prove it was chock full of the usual lunch delicacies: turkey, chips, cookies. What they didn't know was that I made a deal with Calvin: "You carry my lunch for me and I'll give you a piece of the sandwich."

Now that your dog has learned his retrieving exercises, let's teach him the fine art of Carry.

➤ Put a raw potato in a lunch sack.

➤ Put your dog in a Sit.

➤ Fold the top of the bag crisply, turn to your dog and tell him "Carry," as you offer the bag.

➤ When he grasps the bag (which may take him a while in the beginning), praise him, click, and treat. Quit while you're ahead.

➤ An hour or two later, go back and ask him to Carry again, this time stepping back and encouraging him to follow you. When he's taken a step, say "Give," reward, and praise. Repeat this lesson three times.

➤ Next put your dog on a leash and go to a hallway or open area in your house or garage. Present the bag, command "Carry," and walk along five steps. If your dog drops the bag, ignore it and quit. No attention for 15 minutes. (Next time, lower your goal—reward two steps.)

➤ Continue to increase the number of steps until your dog follows you around the house.

Hand Signals

The Carry signal is the same as the Hold signal; point in front of your dog's nose.

➤ Now you're ready to go outside. Start at the potato-in-the-bag step, praising your dog a few steps at a time.

Once your dog reliably carries the bag, you can discourage a distracted drop by saying "Ep, ep," then pointing to the bag. Stay upbeat and positive. No dog wants to carry things for a grump.

When your dog has learned this trick with a bag, he'll want to carry other things, too. He'll insist on helping with the groceries; just give him a cereal box or the buns, tell him "Carry," and off to the kitchen for both of you. When it's time to clean, ask your dog to carry the rag or the paper towels. You'll both be happy.

Fetch the Paper

Wouldn't it be nice to stay inside, cozy in your pajamas, while your best furry friend happily braves the morning cold to fetch your paper? Just be careful what you wish for; a dog who's trained to fetch the paper won't discriminate. You may end up with twenty newspapers on your stoop and twenty angry neighbors!

➤ Fold a section of your newspaper over and tape it securely.

➤ Tempt your dog with it, praising any interest whatsoever.

➤ When your dog lights up to the sight of the paper, begin to command "Fetch the Paper," and let the dog take it in her mouth.

Hand Signals

Whether sending your dog out to get the paper or signaling her to deliver a message, send her off with a happy swoosh!

➤ If your newspaper comes in a plastic bag, introduce it to your dog next. Place the folded (and worn) paper in its plastic bag and repeat the above steps.

Now you can take your show outside. The next morning take your dog with you on-leash. When you come across the paper (which should be similar to the one you've been practicing with indoors), act surprised and point to it, saying "Fetch the Paper." If your dog picks it up, trot back to the house and don't look at her until you're ready to take it. Have a big treat waiting and praise your dog enthusiastically.

When your dog carries the paper back for you, you're ready to start sending her from the door.

➤ Initially, walk within three feet of the paper and say "Fetch the Paper."

➤ If your dog looks confused, run forward, shake the paper playfully, run back, and repeat the command.

➤ Progressively increase your distance from the paper.

➤ Each time your dog returns the paper to you, make a big fuss!

Grrr

Avoid sending your dog out into an unconfined area.
Even the most well-trained dog has one temptation that
will override all his training.

Four-Footed Fax

I was first taught this trick back in college by my big
brother, John. He and his wife have an English Springer
Spaniel named Chelsea who delivers notes to anyone in
the house. Just write out the note, fold it up, tell Chelsea
whom it was meant for, and off she'll go, note in mouth.

Play Hide and Seek (see Chapter 3 for that one) with two
or more people in your house. Equip everyone with a treat
cup. Tell your dog "Go Find Mom" and have mom call
out. When the dog gets to mom, tell him "Go Find Sally"
and have Sally give a yell. And so on. Once your dog
learns who everyone is, you can phase out the yell from
the person being found. Soon your dog will know everyone by name!

Sarah Says

When first playing Hide and Seek, have everyone in visual
range. Slowly start to spread out until everyone is standing
in different areas of the house.

Chapter 12

At Your Service

In This Chapter

➤ Take your dog on laundry patrol

➤ Pick up the trash

➤ Turn out the lights

➤ A helping paw when you sneeze

➤ Send your dog for a soda

Now that you've perfected your dog's retrieving skills, you can put them to work. And, unlike the spouse or the kids, your dog won't think you're a nag; he'll view all the chores as one big game and rush to get started.

Collect the Laundry

The idea of this trick is that when you say "Laundry Round-Up," your dog will go to each room, collect the dirty clothes and put them in the basket. Miraculous! For props, you'll need a plastic laundry basket and some laundry.

Sarah Says

This chapter gets pretty complicated. Clickers really help your dog put it all together. Check Chapter 2 for an explanation of how to use a clicker.

If your dog is a laundry thief, you might be somewhat pessimistic, but hear me out. Laundry bandits are often the top candidates for this task. After all, they're already interested. All you need to do is redirect their efforts. Whatever fetishes are on your retriever's list, you can trust him now because he has learned the exhilaration of sharing his prizes.

You need to start this trick by teaching your dog a few vocabulary words. Get together with a few pieces of clean laundry and the basket. Bring your dog to the basket and say "Round-Up." Next, show him a sock and say "Laundry." Try it a few times and be patient; remember, you're teaching your dog a foreign language.

Now we'll separate the steps. First the laundry. You teach this part standing next to the basket.

➤ Place a sock on the floor three feet away from you and tell your dog "Laundry" as you point to the sock.

➤ If he's clueless, lift it up, put it in his mouth, and run backward repeating "Laundry."

➤ When you get him to bring it back to you, click and praise, letting him drop the sock at your feet.

➤ Continue to practice with laundry items, spread around the room. At first, place one item, then two, then three, sending your dog with the command Laundry each time and clicking and praising each retrieval.

Grrr

Do not handle the sock. Your dog will think laundry means a mouth-to-paw delivery.

Now you're ready to move on to the Round-Up part of this trick.

➤ With your dog at your side and your laundry basket at your feet, give the sock to your dog as you say "Laundry."

➤ Guide his head over the basket as you say "Round-Up" and click simultaneously.

➤ Though you may need a few tries to get it right, click the instant your dog drops the sock into the laundry basket.

➤ Repeat this step until your dog begins to put two and two together.

➤ Now position the laundry three feet away from you. Send your dog by saying "Laundry," and when he gets it say "Round-Up" (you might help a little by pointing to the basket).

➤ Initially, if your dog gets the laundry and brings it over but misses the basket, click to reward his effort. Once he's consistent, only click proper deliveries.

➤ Now try standing across the room from the basket and sending your dog, pointing at the basket and saying "Laundry" and "Round-Up."

➤ Gradually progress to more pieces of laundry in the same room; then aim for a housewide Round-Up.

Sarah Says

Got a small fry? Too small, in fact, to place her head over the Round Up basket? Cut a hole large enough for your dog to fit through into the side of a plastic basket.

Got a big house and rooms and rooms of dirty clothes? You can send your dog out on clothes patrol; just start introducing him to the concept one room at a time. Start your progression in the rooms closest to the Round Up basket and work your way up.

Pick Up the Trash

After your dog has learned how to pick something up and put it in a basket, the possibilities for turning her into a top-notch housekeeper really expand. Picking up the trash is a natural. The goal here is that when you say "Trash It," your dog will go out and pick up whatever trash she sees and put it in a trash can or bag.

Is this another request that leaves you speechless? Has your dog spent most of his life pulling trash out of the bin, rather than putting things in it? Once your pal has learned to retrieve properly, you can trust him around anything, including the garbage.

For props, you'll need a trash bin with a flip top that's sized for your dog. It should be four inches lower than his chin. You'll also need some trash that's safe for him to handle—no sharp edges or food items, please.

Grrr

Never move on to the next step of a trick before your dog has completely mastered the previous step. If you try to rush ahead before your dog is ready, you'll both just end up frustrated and unhappy.

As with all these complex tricks, we'll break this one down and teach it in parts. You start by introducing your dog to the trash can and saying "Trash."

➤ You can encourage your dog's interest in the trash can by rubbing some butter or peanut butter along the inside edge of the lid.

➤ When your dog makes contact with the trash can, click, repeat "Trash," and reward.

➤ Progressively encourage your dog to flip the lid. Remember to click and reward the instant your dog flips the lid.

Your little garbologist! Now that your dog knows how to flip the trash can lid, add some trash. Start with an easy-to-handle trashable like an old Cracker Jack box or, for your small fry, an empty gum wrapper.

➤ Place the garbage on the floor several feet from you and tell your dog "Trash It" as you encourage him to take the item.

➤ When your dog picks the garbage up, step back toward the can, extend your hand for his prize, and click and reward his retrieval. Repeat this step until your dog will go out a distance to retrieve the garbage.

➤ Try introducing more than one piece of garbage.

Now comes the hard part: getting your dog to place the garbage into the can.

➤ Start at the can, leaving the flip lid off. Place the garbage into your dog's mouth and say "Trash It," leaning over the garbage with your clicker.

➤ Your dog will probably look confused. Gently help him place his head over the trash bin (just like you did with the laundry basket). If you find him hopeless and frustrated after a few goes, just be patient.

➤ Click every attempt initially, then fade off and reinforce only those drops that are on target.

➤ Now place trashables around the room and send your dog out for them one at a time, pointing to each object and saying "Trash It." Reinforce each delivery with a click and a treat.

Grrr

Trash bins are often light and flimsy. Weight yours down with several books or rocks in the bottom so it doesn't crash over and frighten your dog.

Now let's finish this trick by getting your dog to push the lid open and drop the garbage in. Sprinkle some trash around the room and don't worry—your pal will take care of it!

➤ Go back to standing next to the trash bin, this time with the flip lid on.

➤ Point to each piece of garbage and instruct your dog to Trash It.

➤ Help him out initially, rewarding each entry. You know he'll catch on eventually.

Turn Out the Light

Do you ever have those moments when you're just too tired to get up and turn out the light? You don't need to rush out and buy The Clapper—your very own Wonder Dog is here. All you have to do is teach him to flip a switch or pull a cord when you say "Lights Out."

This trick has a lot of parts, so be patient. Make Lights Out a project the two of you can work on over time. And remember, the two cardinal rules of trick training are always be patient and always have fun.

Flip the Switch

First you need to teach your dog to put his paws on the wall. Tap the wall, say "Up," and encourage any motions in that direction with clicks and praise. Most dogs catch onto this part pretty quickly, since they love to jump up anyway. (You've already taught your little trickster that jumping is by invitation only, right?)

If your pal is too little to reach the light switch, put a chair against the wall. Pat the chair and tell the dog "Up." Once he's up there, reward him. Now pat the wall and give the Up command again. Got it?

A dog is way more fun than The Clapper!

Keep practicing Up while we move to the next part, which is teaching your dog to use his paw to flip the switch. Remember Paw way back in Chapter 3? Your dog has this one down cold, right? Remind him by asking for Paw in odd places; when your dog is lying down or standing, for example.

Now teach him Paw It by giving the command while you point to something such as a spot on the floor or a piece of paper in your hand. If your dog seems confused when you first ask, hold out your hand in the usual Paw fashion, Paw a bit, then remove it at the last minute. Puppy see, puppy do.

Sarah Says

You may want to cover the area around the light switch with cardboard so your dog doesn't accidentally scratch the wall during training.

Now you're ready for the wall.

➤ Stand right next to the light switch and tell your dog "Up" as you pat the wall, positioning him so his paw is right under the light switch.

➤ Point to the switch and say "Paw It."

➤ Help him turn the switch off by gently guiding his paw. Click and warmly praise whenever he hits the wall in the right area.

➤ Keep practicing, eventually dropping your helping hand but still praising when his paw hits the wall.

➤ Eventually, reward only for correctly pawing the light switch.

Now it's time to add the Lights Out command. Start by linking it to the two commands your dog already knows. Pat the wall and say "Up, Lights Out." Then command "Paw It, Lights Out." When your dog is performing consistently, you can gradually drop the Up and Paw It commands.

Sarah Says

Initially, when your dog is randomly slapping the wall with his paw, flick the light out yourself before you praise him. If you're using a clicker, click the instant the light goes out, whether by paw or hand.

Now you're ready to test your dog when you're not standing at his side. Send him from three feet, then six feet, then across the room—Lights Out! The final test? Send him from the comfort of your bed. Good night.

Pull the Cord

Still have the old pull cords on your lights? Don't worry; your dog can learn this, too. First get a similar pull string and knot the end of it. Dangle it in front of your dog and say "Lights Out." If he reaches for the string, give it a quick tug; then click and reward. Continue this until your dog grabs the string quickly and releases after the tug.

Sarah Says

Is your dog uninterested in your string? Is he thinking you've confused him with your cat? Soak the string in some chicken broth.

This trick also works for a lamp with a pull cord. But to ensure that your dog doesn't pull the string out or send your lamp flying, reward only short tugs. If your dog yanks the cord or tries to "kill" it, say "Ep, ep" and try again. If you're working with a lightweight lamp, secure it before you start practicing.

Now it's time to introduce your dog to the real thing.

➤ Show your dog the light and wave the string.

➤ Say "Lights Out."

➤ When your dog reaches for it, reinforce the behavior by pulling the string yourself, clicking and rewarding.

➤ Progressively reward more and more interaction with the string, always remembering to reward after the light is out, until your dog is pulling the cord himself.

➤ Remember to reward only gentle pulls.

Achoo!

You've got two options with this trick, which basically involves fetching a tissue from the tissue box.

1. When you say "Tissue," your dog will run and get you one.

2. When you sneeze your dog will get you a tissue.

Let me warn you that although the second option is way more impressive, it might leave your dog in a state of career stress. After all, other people sneeze, too.

For props, you'll need a box of tissues, of course. Also, go to your local discount store and get one of those fancy plastic tissue-box containers, so the box will have some resistance when your dog fetches the tissue. (You can also weigh down a regular box, although I had a hard time finding weights small enough.)

Sarah Says

Three key points before you get started:

Secure the box to a low table, using tape or string.

Keep the box in one location; avoid moving it around.

Loosen the tissue for training by pulling it out and lightly restuffing it.

Step one is teaching your dog to put her front paws on the table. Pat the table and give the Up command. Click and reward the instant your dog's front paws hit the table. Be patient; just getting your dog to believe you're inviting her to come up on the table may take a while.

Make sure your dog understands it's front paws only on the table. You can discourage her from bringing the rest of her doggy self along with a gentle "Ep, ep" or even a mild restraint at first.

While I recommend using a low table, even that may not be low enough for your very small trickster. Use a low stool or chair, or even a pillow to help your little dog reach the table. Place the stool between you and your dog, facing her. With treats in hand, command "Up" and pat the stool. If your dog jumps up, reward her immediately. Soon you can say "Up" and point without patting the chair. Then simply follow the preceding steps to teach her to put her paws on the table.

The next part is a classic retrieve; if you're both a little weak on this, just review Chapter 8. Got it? Okay, let's teach your dog how to retrieve a tissue.

Service with a smile when you sneeze.

Kneel on the floor next to your tissue box and say "Tissue," followed by a very theatrical sneeze. As you do this, ruffle the top tissue to pique your dog's interest. Reward her for taking the tissue.

Now your dog has the tissue. Not much help if you need to wipe your nose! But you both know about retrieving, so once your dog takes tissues from you or off the floor, encourage Bring and Give. Reward the instant your dog drops the tissue in your hand.

Once your dog knows the command Tissue and reliably gives it back to you, you're ready to put the whole act together. Sit down and place the tissue box between your knees.

➤ Tell your dog "Get Me a Tissue," or sneeze your most wonderful sneeze and hold out the box.

➤ Reward her the instant she grasps the tissue, the little genius!

➤ Progressively reward only proper tissue pulls, where she pulls the tissue all the way out of the box and drops it in your hand.

➤ Now set the box on the corner of the table (the place it will always be when you do this trick) and repeat the steps I've just outlined. Your dog may need a gentle reminder of "Up," but you can soon phase out that command.

➤ Slowly move yourself farther and farther away from the table. Then request "Get Me a Tissue" standing and sitting in various places in the room. Be sure to reward—and say "Thank you."

Get Me a Soda

I saved the hardest for last. In this one, your long-range goal is that, from anywhere in the house, you can say "Get Me a Soda" and your dog will run to the refrigerator, open it, get a can of soda, close the refrigerator, and bring the soda to you.

It's actually not too tough to teach, if you break it down. Perfect one piece of this trick at a time, and your dog and you will have fun piecing it all together.

Step one is carrying a can. The best way I've found to teach this trick is to first wrap the soda can in a cotton cloth. This is a basic retrieving exercise, and you teach it the same way you taught your dog to retrieve a dumbbell in Chapter 8. First teach your dog to hold the can, then carry it, then bring it to you from a distance—in that order. Each time you present the can, say "Soda." Once your dog is comfortable with the can in her mouth, begin to cut the cloth down piece by piece.

Grrr

Always place the soda cans in the same place. Moving them to another shelf will make it difficult or impossible for your dog to retrieve for you. Also, if you buy a six pack, remove the plastic holding it together and cut it up before you throw it out (the animals of the world will thank you).

Step two is opening the refrigerator. This sounds trickier than it is, although this part, too, needs to be broken down into smaller increments.

➤ Cut a piece of rope long enough so that when it is hung in a loop from the refrigerator door handle, it will hang at the level of your dog's chin.

➤ Let your dog sniff, taste, and otherwise get to know the rope; then secure it to the handle.

➤ Jiggle the rope in front of her nose and command "Get Me."

➤ Click and reward your dog the instant she grasps the rope.

➤ Next, reward a slight pull.

➤ When your dog catches on, reward only when she pulls hard enough to open the door.

Now it's time to teach your dog to remove the can from the fridge.

➤ Wrap the same can you've used for practice back up in the original cloth and place it on a shelf that's roomy enough and high enough for your dog to comfortably grasp it in her mouth.

➤ Prop the refrigerator door open and lead your dog into the kitchen.

➤ Act truly surprised and happy to find the can in the fridge and say "Soda" in a clear, enthusiastic voice. Point the can out if your dog doesn't see it right away.

➤ Reward your dog even if her attempts to retrieve the soda are less than perfect. If she drops it on the ground, encourage her to pick it up.

➤ Continue to practice until your dog is successful at each attempt to get the soda off the shelf.

Now you and your little genius are ready to put it all together. Drumroll please.

➤ Approach the refrigerator with your dog.

➤ Jiggle the rope and *slowly* say "Get Me a . . . "

➤ Wait until your dog is pulling the door open to say "Soda."

➤ If she seems confused, show her the can and say "Soda."

➤ Click and reward the instant your dog gives you the soda. This is the time for jackpot treats. Mission accomplished!

The cutest waiter on earth, and he's all yours!

Now that your dog's figured out all the steps, it's time to test her English comprehension. Stand at the fridge and command "Get Me a Soda." Is she confused? Not sure what all the words mean when they're squashed together? Don't get frustrated. Enunciate each word slowly, and help your dog through the process. Continue to work through this procedure until she's got it mastered.

Progressively extend your distance from the fridge until you can ask your dog from another room. Now imagine lying on the couch, watching the game. You call out "Get Me a Soda," and here comes your dog, can in mouth. She is your best friend!

Chapter 13

Vaudeville Vanities

In This Chapter

➤ Dancing dogs in all their glorious variations

➤ Stringing together several old tricks to make some new ones

➤ Dig a Trench, Run for Cover, Crazy Eights, and more

Now that your dog has discovered her inner talents, is she feeling full of life, full of spirit, full of herself? This chapter is for her—and you. Each of these tricks requires a dog with a strong, outgoing personality and a spitfire attitude about conquering anything new. From disco dog to a theatrical death scene, the dog who masters these tricks will soon be demanding a personal agent.

Dancing Dog

Is your dog just as happy on two paws as she is on four? Is she a ham? A show-off? If your answer is "yes, yes, yes," have I got a trick for you!

If you've got a company jumper, this is also a useful trick; you can teach her that dancing is a better option. When she learns the routine, save it for homecomings or when company calls.

➤ Gather some treats and a clicker, if you have one.

➤ Give your dog a hearty scratch and lots of praise to loosen her up.

➤ Hold a treat at arm's length just inches above your dog's nose.

➤ When she rises to snatch it, say "Dance" and let it go. Do this five times, then quit with a jackpot.

➤ Wait until the next day for lesson two.

➤ Take the treat and hold it just above your dog's nose, as before. But when she reaches up for it, lift it an inch (or more for larger dogs) higher and say "Dance," then let the treat go.

➤ After three days of this routine, begin to say "Dance" as you signal your dog with the treat. Pause, increasing the amount of time before rewarding.

Grrr

Dancing is not a trick for growing pups. It can wreak havoc on their growth plates.

Disco Dog

If your dog loves to jam and you're into disco music, dust off your record collection and clear the floor. You'll never dance alone again (or be kidded about your Bee Gees infatuation).

As you're hustling around, your dog will be getting excited and wondering what part she can play in all this fun. Take one of her treats and say "Dance, Disco," then simply show her the moves you'd like her to imitate. Reward even her simplest efforts. Soon you'll notice that your dog is moving to the grooving.

The Two-Step

Are you a country music buff? There's a dance for you, too. Teach your dog the two-step. When your dog's in the proper dancing position, up on his hind legs, move the treat forward two dog-steps at a time. Be patient if he has a hard time walking at first. You did too.

Grrr

There is one penalty for your Rhythmic Rover: Touching your body, or anyone else's. If your dog bumps into you while dancing, say "Ep, ep" and withdraw the treat. Look up at the ceiling for five seconds, then start again.

May I Have This Dance?

I have a young person in my class with a dog we all call Butter, short for Butterscotch. Butter is a yellow Labrador Retriever who has graduated from a wild and gregarious pup to a fine four-pawed gentleman.

One thing Butter and his owner do when they perfect a routine is dance. But it's not the dancing I've described here. No, they dance the way our parents did, paw-in-arm. It's quite a sight.

Not all dogs qualify for this routine. Your dog must be tall enough, for starters. Sure I dance around with my friend's Pug cradled in my arms, but that's different.

If your dog can reach you at least above your waist, then you have to see if he's willing to keep up with you. Pat yourself and give the Up command you both learned in Chapter 9. Then gently hold your dog's front paws (or place them on your shoulders if you have a Great Dane) and command "Dance." Step back one or two steps at a time and build up slowly. At first, please don't try to make your dog walk backward. And no Waltzes or Tangos on day one.

Grrr

If your dog's a diehard jumper who just can't seem to keep his paws off you, rethink this paw-in-arm dancing routine. Sure, it's fun, but you won't be able to get your little Casanova to stop.

Break Dance

I'll tell you how I discovered this trick. A year ago I was trying to teach Beauty, my Bulldog student, the Down command. Whenever she heard Down she'd flip over, belly up, and twist around like a silly worm. Since it was too hard to get serious with her, I started saying "Break Dance" whenever she'd get started. Before long dear Beauty was break-dancing on command.

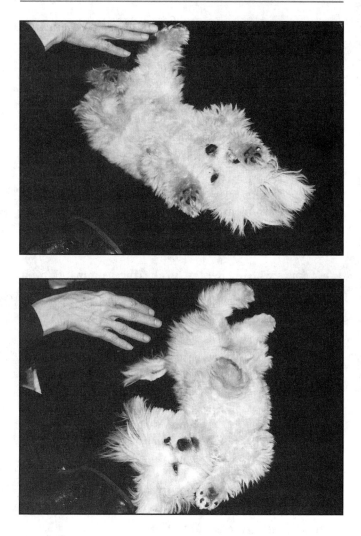

Have you ever seen anything cuter than a Maltese break-dancing?

There's a prerequisite to teaching your dog this command: She must feel comfortable with her feet in the air.

➤ Encourage your dog into the proper Break Dance position by sitting on the floor and scratching her belly.

➤ As soon as those paws are airborne, start waving your hands above her feet and say "Break Dance."

➤ Immediately reinforce your dog with enthusiastic praise and treats. She won't know what you're doing at first, but stick with it. Soon she'll be imitating your movement.

➤ As soon as she catches on, it will be hard to get her to stop.

➤ Now try giving her the Break Dance command from a standing position.

Sarah Says

Small dogs need more security when learning to Break Dance, although they're able to roll around on the floor like the big guys once they learn. Initially, extend your legs in front of you on the floor and sandwich your dog between your calves.

Shoot-Out at the OK Corral

This is where we put together two tricks you learned in Chapter 4: Ask Nicely and Go to Sleep. Together they create a cool stunt that will wow audiences everywhere.

Okay partner, put 'em up!

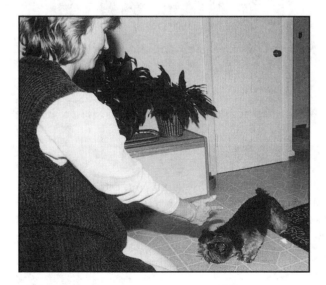

Bang!

First, get your dog to sit up (Ask Nicely), adding a command such as "Put 'Em Up." Make the shape of a gun with your thumb and index finger and point it at her. Practice that quite a few times.

Remember that the way to teach a new command for an old trick is to first link them, then phase out the old command. So when your dog starts, you'll give her the commands "Ask Nicely, Put 'Em Up." Emphasize the new hand signal, and slowly eliminate the Ask Nicely command.

Once your dog is sitting up, it's time for the Go to Sleep command. Link it with "Bang" as you "pull the trigger" on your hand gun. If she has trouble, gently help her over to her side. Often the dog will get so excited that she will fall down anyway. Practice the two steps together several times, rewarding for each improvement and phasing out Go to Sleep.

Now to put it all together.

➤ Put your dog in a Sit-Stay.

➤ Stand three feet away and command "Put 'Em Up" as you take aim.

➤ Pause a few seconds and say "Bang."

➤ Mission accomplished! Now practice at progressively farther distances.

Dig a Trench

Have you considered hiring out your dog to the local excavating company? The answer, of course, is to teach her to dig. By teaching your dog to dig in specific locations, you'll be able to discourage her from digging in other places. Sound too good to be true?

➤ Equip yourself with a clicker, garden gloves, and treats.

➤ Find a private area in your yard or a local park to teach your dog to dig. Bury some treats one inch under the ground to pique her interest.

➤ Start blissfully digging yourself, unearthing the treats as you go and handing them to your dog.

➤ Reward your dog for joining in, saying "Go Dig."

➤ Now try hiding a few treats or a toy before bringing your dog to her digging spot. Like an archeologist discovering treasures, she'll unearth them with obvious delight.

Sarah Says

I can already feel the page trembling; some of you are worried that, with your approval, your dog will dig up your shrubbery and carpets. Though I won't promise you a rose garden, most dogs who are reinforced for digging in one area usually stick to it.

Run for Cover

Once your dog knows this trick she'll use it all day long, just to get your attention.

To begin, use a treat to lead your dog under the object you want her to go under (for this example we'll use a table). Each time, use the command Under. Practice this step periodically throughout the day.

Run for cover.

Now send her under the table with "Under" and command "Stay." Release her with "Okay" and a great big hug. Gradually increase the amount of time before the release.

Ready to put it all together? Get some treats and your clicker, if you have one.

➤ After sending your dog Under and instructing her to Stay, say "Peekaboo" as you use a treat to lure just your dog's nose out from under the table.

➤ Click and release the treat when your dog's nose is the only thing showing.

➤ If she has her whole head out, lure her head back under the table and start again.

It may take some practice to master the perfect Peekaboo, but once learned it's never forgotten.

The delicious Peekaboo!

Injured Dog

Although there are many steps to this trick, it's not too complicated when broken down.

➤ Gather your clicker and treats.

➤ With your dog on-leash, give the Sit command.

➤ Next, command "Paw" (your Chapter 3 favorite, right?) as you hold the index finger of your left hand under her forearm.

➤ Simultaneously, introduce the leash under her paw with your right hand.

➤ Next command "Stand" (you learned that one in Chapter 2 as Stand Here, Stand There), then "Paw." Introduce the injured dog hand signal.

➤ If your dog's confused, lift the left paw gently with your leash. Click and reward the second your dog has her paw in the air.

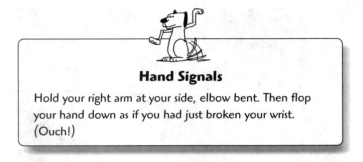

Hand Signals

Hold your right arm at your side, elbow bent. Then flop your hand down as if you had just broken your wrist. (Ouch!)

Practice this part of the trick a lot. Got it? Okay, on to the finished production.

➤ Command "Stand," then "Paw" (give the hand signal), cradling your dog's paw with the leash.

➤ Step two feet away from her and command "Come," still supporting her paw.

➤ Remind her that her paw still needs to be off the floor by giving the hand signal several times throughout the Come. Click and reward her for a job well done.

Crazy Eights

This trick is fun for you to teach and fun for dogs of all shapes and sizes to learn. What could possibly be better than that?

➤ Start from the Heel position, take a giant step forward with your right foot only, then freeze. Point between your legs and use a treat to encourage your dog to come "Through."

➤ Once your dog has perfected Through, use the treat to lead your dog once around your legs in a figure-eight pattern, ending up back in the Heel position.

(Obviously, you'll have to rely solely on the lure of the treat; using a leash to lead your dog would leave you both hopelessly tangled!)

Hand Signals

Point between your legs.

Once your dog has perfected Through, use the treat to lead him in a figure-eight pattern.

Repeat this step until you're sure your dog knows it well.

➤ To put it all together, do the same routine but walk forward extremely slowly.

➤ Each time your dog circles a leg, move the opposite leg forward.

➤ If that's okay with her, pick up the pace; if not, go back a step and perfect that.

➤ After some practice, she'll be tripping you and bringing the crowds to tears with laughter.

Sarah Says

If your dog's having trouble, do one part at a time. First through the middle, then around the right leg . . . reward. Then through the middle again . . . reward, and so on. Practice this until she does it very well.

Chapter 14

The Impressionist

In This Chapter

➤ Teach your dog to roll over, flip and catch a treat, and crawl

➤ Balancing a book on the dog's head

➤ Expanding your trick repertoire by using hand signals

Animal acts always make people smile, especially when they're all performed by your animal. Some of these impressions your friends will easily guess. Others will be even more funny if you announce the impression first.

The Dolphin

Who has not seen a dolphin do a perfect water roll at an aquarium or a water park? Your dog, while not as fluid in her movements, can still do a pretty fair likeness. To get started, place your clicker and treats on a nearby table.

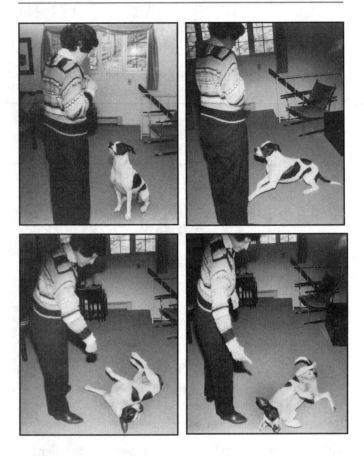

Teach your dog to do the roll, fluid as a dolphin.

➤ Call your dog to you and put her on a Down-Stay.

➤ Scratch your dog's belly until she lies on one side.

➤ Take a treat and hold it above your dog's ear. Now circle it slowly backward over the back of her head as you say "Roll Over."

➤ Initially your dog may need some help. Guide her over by gently pushing her top front leg to the other side as you say the command. Click and treat a full roll, whether you helped your dog or not.

➤ Repeat this four times a session, then quit on a high note with your dog's favorite game.

Once your dog seems able to follow the command, you can teach her to jump up after each roll. For this all you need is a little bit of enthusiastic body language and up she goes. Initially you should reward the roll; then reward the roll and finish.

Now you're ready to teach your dog the hand signal for this trick. Continue to kneel next to her when commanding Roll Over, but lean backward (in the direction you want her to roll), hold your index finger parallel to the floor, and draw small circles in the air as you give your verbal command. Help your dog initially if she seems confused, praising her as you assist and jumping up with her to end the trick. Once she responds alone, stand up and give the command and the hand signal, always accentuating your hand signal.

Grrr

This is a very entertaining trick, but please don't force your dog if she's not into it. Some dogs love to act silly; others don't. How will you know? If your dog shifts from side to side with ease, if she rolls around on her own, she'll be game. If rolling around on the floor is beneath her standards, don't force it.

Once your dog has learned the hand signal, you're ready for control at a distance.

> ➤ Place your dog in a Down-Stay and stand back three feet. Use your hand signal, leaning your body in the direction you're sending your dog, as you command "Roll Over."

> ➤ If your dog looks confused, go to her calmly and help out, getting back into your starting position as she finishes the trick.

> ➤ When she performs on her own, give her a jackpot of treats and end with a fun game.

> ➤ Back up two feet at a time during your subsequent practice sessions, until your dog will Roll Over at a reasonable distance from you.

The Seal

In this one, you teach your dog to balance a treat on her nose, then flip it up, and catch it. Sound hard? We've all seen seals do this with a fish. And surely your pup is smarter than a seal!

You'll need to break this one into two parts: the balance, and the flip and catch.

Balancing Act

> ➤ Line up treats and your clicker on a nearby table.

> ➤ Put your dog on a Sit-Stay.

> ➤ Gently hold your dog's nose steady for five seconds, reminding "Stay" if she gets squeamish. Click and reward just that. Repeat five times. The first lesson is over.

> ➤ Later that day or the next day, repeat the above lesson, but place a treat on your dog's nose while you steady it, reminding "Stay."

➤ After five seconds, say "Okay," removing the treat that's on her nose and rewarding her with a different treat. Do not reward your dog with the treat on her nose.

➤ Repeat this exercise four times, then stop for the day.

➤ Continue to practice this step until your dog is proficient at balancing the treat on her nose for at least fifteen seconds, no nose-holding required.

Flip and Catch

Teach this part only after perfecting the balance.

➤ Balance a treat on your dog's nose, then introduce the next concept by saying "Okay" as you slide the treat from your dog's nose to her mouth.

➤ After a day or two, you should notice that your dog tries to flip the treat herself. Praise her only if her flip follows your "Okay."

➤ If she flips prematurely, say "Ep, ep" and practice the balance alone a few times before continuing.

Now you're ready to put the whole trick together.

➤ Balance the treat and command "Stay."

➤ Walk back three feet and pause. Vary the length of your pauses as you practice.

Sarah Says

To help your dog learn to wait for your Okay before flipping the treat, vary the balance time before sliding the treat into her mouth.

Once your dog knows how to balance a treat, he's ready to learn the Flip and Catch.

➤ Say "Okay" for the catch and make a big fuss when she does, praising your dog with lots of love.

The Snake

This trick always amazes me, and it's fairly easy to teach. Your dog must be proficient in Down, but if you've gotten this far I'll take that for granted.

➤ Gather up your treats and a clicker.

➤ Give your dog the Down command.

➤ Hold a treat in front of his nose and bring it forward slowly so he has to stretch. As he does, say "Crawl."

➤ Progressively encourage your dog to move forward.

➤ The first few days you should reinforce one crawl step at a time.

➤ If you're having trouble teaching this one, lie in front of your dog and extend your hand so that it just reaches his nose.

➤ Wiggle your hand forward as if it were a mouse in the grass, again reinforcing the smallest attempt to reach for the treat.

➤ Once your dog will crawl forward 10 feet (this might take a few weeks), begin giving your dog the Crawl command from a kneeling position.

➤ Finally, stand up and say "Crawl" as you signal him forward, wiggling your hand in front of him.

Sarah Says

If your dog is having trouble keeping her belly planted on the floor, lay your right hand across her shoulder blades and apply the least amount of pressure possible.

Think you're hot stuff? Then try this crawl routine.

➤ Place your dog in a Down-Stay and stand three feet in front. Instead of calling her, kneel down and say "Crawl."

➤ Release her with "Okay" the moment she gets to you, and celebrate. Job well done! Now you can work at getting her to crawl to you across the room. Good luck.

Eliza Doolittle

Okay, this is not an animal trick. But it is still an impression. Do you remember the scene in My Fair Lady when Eliza Doolittle walks around the living room with a book balanced on her head? This is the same trick, only your dog is going to do it. As usual, let's break this trick down into its significant parts.

Stand Still

Here's a quick refresher course, in case your dog has forgotten the art of standing still.

➤ Kneel down on the floor next to your dog.

➤ Place your right hand, palm out, under your dog's buckle collar.

➤ Slide your left hand under your dog's belly.

➤ Command "Stand-Stay" as you gently prop your dog into a standing position.

➤ Relax your right hand and slide your left to rest on your dog's thigh.

➤ Pause, count to five, and release with an Okay.

➤ Slowly increase the time to one minute.

➤ Now repeat the same sequence from a standing position.

➤ Begin to let go with your left hand, then your right, as you steady your dog with calm Stay commands and a relaxed posture.

Once your dog catches on, you'll find a million uses for this command: wiping muddy paws, brushing, a towel dry, an Eliza Doolittle imitation . . . .

Hand Signals

The hand signal for Stand Still is a level hand, arm extended, palm up.

Slow Down

This is another little trick that I'm sure you can think of a million uses for. Plus, your dog can't possibly balance a book on his head and fly across the room at the same time. Let's slow it down!

To get started you'll need two people: one to lead the dog forward and one to hold him back.

➤ Position yourself in front of your dog with treats. Place your partner behind the dog, holding a leash attached to your dog's buckle collar.

➤ Using your Stay signal, command "Stand-Stay." If your dog moves, reposition her calmly and quietly.

➤ To signal your dog to move forward, close your fingers, move your hand forward and say "Slowly."

➤ After each step, reward your dog with a treat as your assistant pulls gently back to stop the dog from taking more than one step at a time.

➤ Repeat this until your dog begins to slow after each step on her own; no tug necessary.

➤ Now see if you can do it without a partner, using Shhh if your dog is too excited. One step at a time.

➤ Now try it at a distance. Leave your dog in a Stand-Stay and stand three feet in front of her. Command

and signal "Slowly," and praise your dog for moving with caution.

Balancing the Book

This next step is a big one. If your dog's not ready for it, slow up yourself.

Consider the type of book you use. Paperbacks sag and don't balance well. Avoid books with jackets or glossy covers—too slippery. A bare, hardcover book works best. Also, use a book that doesn't weigh too much and that suits the size of your dog; your Chihuahua may only be able to handle a book of postage stamps.

➤ To help your dog learn to balance a book, you will have to steady her head so the book rests evenly. Do this by gently holding her muzzle with your right hand, giving the Stay signal with your left hand in front of her nose and repeating "Stay."

➤ At first, click and reward after just a few seconds, building the duration slowly over many days.

➤ When your dog begins to learn the routine, lift your right hand off her muzzle ever so slightly as you leave the Stay signal in place and remind "Stay."

Sarah Says

Is your dog letting the book slide? Either you're going too fast or your dog is following you with her eyes as you step away. Help her keep her focus steady by holding the hand signal for Stay steady at her nose level, then moving it slightly up or down if she needs recentering.

➤ Slowly increase the time your dog can balance the book without your help and the distance you can move from her.

Putting It All Together

If I had to pick the toughest trick in the book, this would be it. So drumroll, please.

Here goes.

➤ Standing close to your dog, place her in a Stand position and tell her "Stay."

➤ Place the book on her head, remind "Stay" and step away two feet.

➤ Keeping your Stay signal level with your dog's nose, command "Slowly" and give the hand signal.

➤ Immediately remove the book after one step, click and reward. Quit on a high note and go for a walk.

➤ Work on this step for a few days to build your dog's confidence. Progress to two steps, then three, four, five . . . .

➤ Now send me a picture of your dog imitating Eliza Doolittle for the next printing of this book.

The Neighbor's Dog

This one's my favorite. Once your dog knows the hand signal for Speak, you can say "What does the neighbor's dog do?" give the signal, and your dog will bark, bark, bark.

This is a pretty funny trick, and it illustrates an important concept about hand signals: Once your dog can respond to your signals, it won't matter what you're saying. Your dog will react to the signal alone.

When you feel confident about your hand signals, you can borrow other tricks from this book to do more impressions. For example, Wolf is just the Howl command, and Dancing Bear is easily done using one of the many dance routines you learned in Chapter 10.

If you want to tack on a verbal command, hook the new command onto the old (for example, Howl-Wolf) while emphasizing your hand signal.

Chapter 15

Pet Detective

In This Chapter

➤ Teaching Sniff and Find

➤ Discriminating between toys

➤ Find the keys, the remote, and anything else you can think of

---

Initially I had a hard time deciding which chapter to end the trick section with. But I decided to save the best for last. Your dog doesn't need to be a miraculous retriever or double-jointed to succeed in Doggy Detective School. The only prerequisites are a curious nose and an enthusiastic heart.

Sniff and Find

To train a good detective, you must start with the basics. What better way to get that sniffer going than with some tasty treats?

Stage One

➤ Gather some smell-good treats, go to a large room or hallway, and place your dog in a Sit-Stay.

➤ Say "Sniff" as you hold a treat in front of your dog's nose.

➤ Discourage any test-tasting with "Ep, ep."

➤ Remind "Stay," toss the treat no more than three feet in front of you, and make your dog wait.

➤ Release with "Okay, Find."

➤ Praise your dog for locating and gobbling the treat.

➤ Gradually extend your toss to not more than 10 feet. Once your dog perfects this part of the trick, move on to the next stage.

Sarah Says

Always vary the time you pause your dog, so he won't jump the gun. Pause three seconds, ten seconds, fourteen, or twenty—mix it up. This will encourage your dog to concentrate on your commands.

Stage Two

➤ Command "Sniff" and "Stay" as before, but leave your dog's side and place the treat inches in front of him.

➤ Return to your dog's side, pause, and release with "Okay, Find."

➤ Gradually extend your distance to not more than fifteen feet. At this point, your dog may lose sight of the treat and have to rely on his sniffer to find it.

Stage Three

Now you're ready to put your four-footed detective to the test.

➤ Place your dog on a Stay four feet from the entrance to the room.

➤ Instruct "Sniff," remind "Stay," and place your treat out of sight around the corner.

➤ Return to your dog, pause, and then send him off with "Okay, Find."

➤ Cheer him on if he seems confused. You may have to get on all fours yourself and sniff around, though you should praise him enthusiastically regardless of how he locates the treat.

Sarah Says

This was my dog Kyia's favorite game. I used vegetables, hiding four or five while I was making a salad, just to keep her busy.

Once your dog has the idea and is racing to put his nose to work, you can progressively hide the treat in more challenging places. And who's to say that you have to hide just one?

Find Your Toy

Now let's progress to finding something just as fun but a little less tasty: toys. For this you'll need a clicker if you use one, some good treats, and two distinctly different toys. I'll use a ball and a little stuffed cow toy, but you can use whatever toys your dog loves.

➤ Start with the ball. Hold it in front of your dog, clicker in the other hand and treats lined up on a nearby table.

➤ Say "Find Your Ball" as you hold the ball in front of your dog. When he reaches for it, click, treat, and praise.

➤ Repeat a few times, then tell your dog "Stay" as you place the ball a few feet in front of him. Repeat "Find Your Ball" as you point to it. Click and reward any contact.

➤ Continue to move the ball farther from you and progress to hiding it out of sight.

➤ Practice that trick for a week, then start the whole routine from scratch with the cow. The command should be "Find Your Cow."

Sarah Says

Though I encourage you to use treats initially to motivate your dog, you'll be able to phase them out as soon as your dog gets a mental image of what you're expecting.

That was the easy part. Now we're going to make it a little harder.

➤ With your dog in a Sit-Stay, place both toys in front of him, about three feet apart.

➤ Command "Find Your Cow."

➤ If your dog picks the ball, don't correct him or sound disappointed. Calmly take the toy, replace it, show your dog the cow, and say "Cow." When he makes contact, click and reward.

➤ If your dog picks the cow, make a big fuss; what a genius!

➤ Practice this a few times at each session, sometimes sending the dog for the ball and sometimes for the cow. (Don't alternate them; that's too easy and your dog will quickly catch on.)

➤ Progressively place the toys farther away.

Once your dog has mastered the art of association, you're ready to test his brain some more. Place one toy three feet from you, and the other ten feet away. Send your dog for the closer one at first, and then send him for the one farthest away. Switch the toys' locations and vary which one you send him to.

At this point you can apply the dog's discrimination abilities to other objects, as I'll discuss here.

Find the Keys

How much time do you spend around your house looking for your keys? It would be great if you could just send your little genius detective after them, wouldn't it? Here's how:

➤ Line up some treats, grab the keys, and round up the clicker if you use one.

➤ Place your dog in a Sit-Stay and let him sniff the keys as you say "Sniff."

➤ Toss the keys a few feet out and instruct "Find the Keys." If your dog makes contact, click immediately and reward. If not, help him out by guiding him or shaking the keys, and click the second he catches on.

➤ Progressively extend the distance you toss the keys in front of you. When your dog really learns this part, you can start to hide the keys in another room.

➤ When you hide the keys, do it in plain sight and follow your dog while he searches. Reinforce with a click and/or a treat the second he locates them.

Sarah Says

Do you leave your keys all over the house? Perhaps you should consider spraying your key chain with your perfume from time to time. The better to sniff it out.

Where's the Remote?

This is, perhaps, the most often-asked question in America. And your doggy detective always knows the answer!

By this time your dog should know Sniff and Find. Line up the treats and your clicker, and let's get to work.

➤ Let your dog have a good sniff of the remote, enhancing its smell with something memorable such as baby powder.

➤ Leave him in a Stay and place the remote a few feet away.

➤ Release your dog with "Find the Remote" and reinforce any contact.

➤ Continue to increase the distance, then begin to hide it in the usual lost-remote locations.

Sarah Says

Is your dog an expert retriever? You can have your Private Eye retrieve the object once he's found it. Praise the Find and then encourage Bring.

Find Bobby

Have kids? Ever lose them? In the house, outside, at the neighbor, or elsewhere? Pet Detective to the rescue.

Start with one child, whom I'll call Bobby.

➤ Place Bobby across the room with a treat cup.

➤ Take your dog across the room and say "Find Bobby."

➤ When Bobby hears his name, he should shake the treat cup.

➤ When your dog goes to Bobby, Bobby should reward him with a treat.

➤ Repeat as often as necessary, until the shaking of the cup is no longer necessary to encourage your dog to find Bobby. During the training process, Bobby should offer a treat whenever he's found.

➤ Now hide Bobby in the next room. Start back at the beginning where Bobby shakes the cup when he hears his name.

➤ Extend your distance to other rooms and locations until your dog is proficient at finding Bobby wherever he's hiding.

➤ Now practice outdoors, first with Bobby close by and eventually with Bobby behind a tree or somewhere out of sight.

➤ You can start adding kids one at a time, until your dog knows everyone in the neighborhood.

Snoop Doggy Dog

Though your dog won't be able to find you a refund on your taxes, he can learn to find just about anything you can lose. Dogs are able to associate plenty of objects with words. Just follow the basic framework for the tricks taught in this chapter, and initially rely on treats to reinforce his success.

Here are some other everyday things you may want to teach your dog to scout out: your slippers, the cat (you know the cat is going to love this one!), your other mitten—be creative. What gets lost in your home? Now, tell it to your dog. Pet Detective to the rescue!

Chapter 16

Happy Tails to You

In This Chapter

➤ Your dog's true worth

➤ What we all learn from dogs

Sure your dog may never star in a commercial or he may be too embarrassed to show off his routines at the local Elks Club, but that doesn't rob you of the one undeniable fact: If you love your dog, he's a star. And the size of your star is not measured by how many people share your pride, it's measured by you.

When I listen to some of my friends and clients talk about their dogs, whether it be a tale of mischief or one of training, I feel the warmth in their hearts, and when I see the dog face-to-face I already know that dog's worth.

Canine Ambassador

I always say, a well-trained dog is an ambassador for us all. Whether you're just clowning around in your living room or you're putting on an act at a local fair, the work and time you've devoted to your dog will shine through wherever you take him.

You'll be surprised at the doors you will be able to open with the simplest of tricks. Children, otherwise terrified of dogs, will delight in a well-mannered trickster. People with no time for the four-footed will look on in wonder. And those of us who love our dogs as much as you do will congratulate you on your efforts toward making the world a more dog-friendly place.

Strictly Optional, Strictly Fun

Many people have asked me why I decided to write this book. An editor and old friend of mine even went so far as to warn me off the project, saying that a book about tricks would hurt my reputation as a serious trainer. Too late now!

Reputation or not, I gave my editor the same answer I give everyone else: I wrote this book for the fun of it. It was fun for me; I needed a break from the heel and housebreaking. And hopefully, it has been fun for you. After all, having fun with your dog usually tops the list of reasons we share our lives with dogs in the first place.

They bring us back to a time when pleasure was our only priority, when having a good time and being loved unconditionally was the name of the game.

I guess the most special thing about writing this book, what makes it different from the other training books I've written, is that this one is optional. Nobody has to teach their dog tricks. After all, it's time consuming and requires incredible patience and understanding. But if you have chosen to go this extra mile, I know that your relationship with your dog is a special one, unique from all the others. Your dog is your gift, and in turn you have chosen to give back to him.

Happy tails to you. 'Til we meet again!

That's me with some of my star pupils.

More to Read

General Care and Training

Burnham, Patricia Gail, *Playtraining Your Dog,* New York: St. Martins Press, 1980.

Carlson, Delbert, DVM and James Giffin, MD, *Dog Owner's Home Veterinary Handbook,* New York: Howell Book House, 1992.

DeBitetto, James, DVM and Sarah Hodgson, *You and Your Puppy,* New York: Howell Book House, 1995.

Hodgson, Sarah, *The Complete Idiot's Guide to Choosing, Training, and Raising a Dog,* New York: Alpha Books, 1996.

Hodgson, Sarah, *DogPerfect,* New York: Howell Book House, 1995.

Trick Training

Baer, Ted, *How to Teach Your Old Dog New Tricks,* Hauppauge, NY: Barron's, 1991.

Benjamin, Carol Lea and Capt. Arthur Haggerty, *Dog Tricks,* New York: Howell Book House, 1987.

Pryor, Karen, *Don't Shoot the Dog!,* New York: Bantam Books, 1984.

Zeigenfuse, Mary Ann and Jan Walker, *Dog Tricks, Step by Step,* New York: Howell Book House, 1997.

Videos

Hobdy, Ruth, *Control Exercises,* United States Dog Agility Association, 1991.

Hodgson, Sarah, *DogPerfect,* Cooperative Canine Corp., 1996.

Owens, Mary, *The ABC's of Dog Training,* Canine University, Pensacola, Florida.

Take a Bow Wow, *Take a Bow Wow,* 1995.

Index